World Cup 2018

WORLD CUP 2018

An Armchair Fan's Guide

Lloyd Pettiford and **Ronan Fitzsimons**

Urbane
PUBLICATIONS

First published in Great Britain in 2018 by Urbane Publications Ltd
Suite 3, Brown Europe House, 33/34 Gleaming Wood Drive, Chatham, Kent
ME5 8RZ

Copyright © Lloyd Pettiford and Ronan Fitzsimons, 2018

A CIP catalogue record for this book is available from the British Library.

ISBN 978-1-912666-09-6

MOBI 978-1-912666-10-2

Design and Typeset by The Invisible Man

Cover by Julie Martin

Printed and bound by 4edge Limited, UK

Urbane
PUBLICATIONS
urbanepublications.com

With thanks to

Matthew Smith, David Harding, Steve Kneller, Rod Besseling, Patrick Devitt and Peter Wilkin.

Contents

Preamble   ix

Introduction   xi

Le World Cup History   1

The Road to Russia: Qualification   27

Summary of who did Qualify   42

Qualifiers by Group (without any Veneer of Seriousness)   49

You're Not Singing Anymore   131

Conclusions   143

Appendix (Fixtures etc)   148

Preamble

concerning teams ranked #187=, #191 and #200 in the world by FIFA

The road to Russia took in 871 qualifiers and began, over three years before the tournament kick-off, in strangely symbolic fashion. First, East Timor thrashed Mongolia 4-1. A creditable performance, you might imagine. Indeed Timor Leste followed that up with a 0-1 victory in Ulaan Baatar leading to boundless enthusiasm in the comments section of FIFA's website and dreams of qualification for the giant-killers from Dili. However, hats-off to one Mongolian fan who after the first leg defeat prophesised: "I believe in Mongolia. 3-0 against Timor Leste [in the home leg] and 2nd round for Mongolia!! [on away goals rule]" The thing is, East Timor 'inadvertently' included a number of Brazilians in their team who were ineligible to play and so both legs of the tie were awarded 3-0 to Mongolia, who progressed as predicted. Except, Timor Leste then appear in the second round results not Mongolia? Many of their games appear to have been forfeited 0-3 (including 1-1 draws against Malaysia and Palestine) so Mongolia's 'triumph' appears only retrospective and the discovery of East Timor's trickery somewhat tardy. Anyway, let's leave that to forensic football fans to fathom, except to mention that Timor Leste's 0-10 spanking at the hands of Saudi Arabia *does* appear to have counted, including Mohammed Al Sahlawi knocking in five. Might be worth a flutter as first goal-scorer in the opener against Russia, bearing in mind the teams' respective world rankings? Confused? Cheating? FIFA?! Strangely symbolic? Whatever could we mean...

But of course there are other, err beautiful, sides to the beautiful game. Enter Bhutan, whose qualifiers against Sri Lanka now became the first qualifiers in the light of the expunging of East Timorese results. Travelling to Colombo as FIFA's officially worst ranked team, Bhutan pulled off a fine 0-1 win thanks to a late Dorji strike. Excitement was high therefore for the return in oxygen-starved Thimphu, Bhutan's high altitude Capital (and only) City. The official crowd was reported as 15,000, but the strictly impartial BBC correspondent suggests 30,000 squeezed in, to see Bhutan win 2-1 and progress to the second round group qualifiers. Although Bhutan lost all eight matches (including 15-0 to Qatar and 12-0 to China) they are nonetheless now firmly ensconced in the top 200 in the world ahead of Tonga, Gibraltar, San Marino, Timor Leste and many others. They also scored three goals in the last five minutes against the Maldives in their cauldron-like Changlimithang Stadium, almost pulling off a remarkable recovery, but losing 3-4.

Introduction

& A Caveat Concerning Travel to Russia: Please Don't Go! (We're begging you to stay)

I have previously written guides to major football tournaments in 2002 (tri-authored), 2004 (single authored) and 2016 (co-authored, with Ronan as now). Some criticism of these endeavours has come from those who seemed to miss the point entirely of something the publisher was careful to describe as 'irreverent'. Complaint seemed to centre on the fact that whilst the aim was to provide historical, qualification and team information in a mildly amusing fashion, people had somehow hoped for *Lonely Planet*-style advice including the best place to buy a *crêpe and cheeky chablis* before the match, the locations of *pensions* and *estaminets* and so on. So, if you want a *Lonely Planet* guide to Russia, I believe Lonely Planet does actually produce one. Let us be quite clear on the content of this book, however. It is an informed, occasionally ridiculous, analysis of the World Cup in Russia. It absolutely invites you to put it next to you on the sofa and not go to Russia. When Morocco v South Korea looks like no-one will ever score, you'll be grateful.

So, why should you not go to Russia? Apart, that is, from the sour grapes argument that the 2018 World Cup should be taking place in England anyway...is that not enough for you then? Well there are also the Foreign and Commonwealth advisories against travel to certain parts of Russian territory and the experiences of friends who have previously travelled to Moscow for football (see below). And Russian thugs have stepped up their game since then, whatever Hull City's Russian ex-manager may say. I hesitate to give Russian hooligans more oxygen, so I won't repeat any of their silly gang names, or quote them very much. Needless to say, they have silly gang names and laugh at the idea that any male visiting the tournament is not a fair target; they will be, regardless of behaviour. They see themselves as defending Russian honour and have been congratulated by politicians for doing so. They train for violence for violence's sake, don't drink accordingly and often express neo-Nazi sentiment. If we don't go, not only will that send a strong message to Russia, but the hooligans will undoubtedly fight amongst themselves. You have been warned, not by us, but by them.

But 'Stay at home' is not an exclusively health and safety argument. A political one could be made for all sorts of reasons: you might want to boycott Russia in protest at the corruption in FIFA and Russian sport more generally. Or to express solidarity with writers and journalists in Russia who find themselves bumped off or in prison for challenging authority and having dissident opinion. You may be concerned by the fact that Russia is still, nearly 30 years on from the days of the USSR, a fundamentally dysfunctional, antidemocratic, racist and homophobic society (and so on), with crazy friends in the White House (allegedly). And there's the hazing in the Russian military and other possible human rights abuses too. But this is not the time and place for any of those arguments, and if anyone with a fur hat and an umbrella asks, it wasn't me that made them, right.[1]

But the main reason for not suggesting, as I did with Portugal and France, that you dust off the phrase book and make the travel reservations, is simply that we believe you'll have a better time on your sofa with our book. We should stress that this argument does depend to some extent on you also having a piece of televisual equipment, or at the very least a wireless. If you haven't, take our book to the pub. Although Moscow and St Petersburg, for instance, are *in places* rather beautiful cities where many locals will genuinely welcome you, Russia will be expensive. Local poverty will encourage people to make a buck out of gullible, drunk foreigners. Not all locals are renowned for their friendliness and, especially if France 2016 is anything to go by, some of them may be looking to make an organised point in confronting foreign fans, particularly those from England. Finally, xenophobic tendencies may be added to by other prejudice, especially if you are black or gay. And imagine the take-aways and beer you can buy if you don't have hotels, flights, car-hire and tickets to worry about.

So, if this guide will not take you from the expensive restaurants of St Petersburg, to non-functioning air-con in Sochi to pick-pockets and vodka outlets in Moscow, what will it do? The answer is: anything at all for a cheap laugh which doesn't involve travelling to Russia. In actual fact, I have never been to Russia, but the fact that I have managed to form opinions like those above is probably the reason why. So, thanks for buying the book, and if you are going to Russia, leave it at home. It'll get you (and us) into nothing but trouble.

---

[1] I might be even less enthusiastic about a World Cup in the USA at the moment, but that's another story.

From Russia Without Much Love: A Fan's Experience

Steve, real name *Steve*, had always wanted to go to see the sights of Moscow and England were playing there in European qualifiers in 2008. A charter flight, a couple of days' sight-seeing and the footie... what could be better? Trying to wash your private parts using sand, probably.

All England fans were due to be staying in the same hotel: a huge place that had in fact been the Olympic village for the 1984 Moscow Olympics. Russian hooligans got wind of this and were planning a reception committee. This gave Russian police a problem, not to mention work they hadn't anticipated. However, they had a cunning plan. Russian air-traffic control denied landing permission for charter flights for thirteen hours. This gave Steve, and all the other England fans, the opportunity to spend money on over-priced everything at the sumptuous Luton Airport and to get a view of Moscow only very late in the day and in darkness.

Check in at the hotel was horrendous and included the taking in of all passports to be checked by the lovely local constabulary. So after a not very long night's sleep, job number one was a huge queue to get passports back after the huge queue to check in. Some people decided to go out and explore and get their passports back later. This resulted in $100 fines from the police outside the hotel for not carrying the appropriate papers. Do not expect these guys to protect or serve you. Having recovered his passport, Steve was eager to make the most of things and had organised a sight-seeing tour. The Kremlin looked nice, though Lenin's mausoleum was by that time closed. Steve, a multi-lingual culture vulture and vegetarian, was keen to see some of the less well known aspects of the city... however, the only other 'sight' they were shown was the 'first McDonalds to open in Moscow'. If this was an important symbolic moment in the story of *glasnost* and *perestroika*, and the end of the Soviet Union, Steve was nonetheless unimpressed.

And so to the game itself. England led 0-1 at half-time but conceded two goals in five second-half minutes and lost. After the game Steve, dispirited and poorer, was put onto a coach and taken to the airport. This could all be yours...oh, and you might get beaten up too.

World Cup 2018

Le World Cup History[1]

The brain child of two Frenchmen (Jules Rimet and Henri Delauney), the World Cup got FIFA backing in 1928 and after Uruguay offered to pay other teams' expenses, it kicked off in 1930 in **Uruguay**. France, Yugoslavia, Belgium and Romania travelled from Europe to join eight (mostly Latin) American sides. Highlights were:

- France beat Mexico 4-1 captained by Alex Villaplane, later executed by *la résistance* for collaborating with the Nazis
- Romania beat Peru 3-1 in front of the lowest ever World Cup crowd, estimated at 300
- Belgium travelled all that way and failed to score
- Mario de las Casas (Peru) was the first player to be sent off at a World Cup
- Despite Brazil being part of the tournament it was Argentina, Uruguay and the USA which made up the Americas semi-final representatives
- Europe's sole survivors were the Yugoslavs

The USA team included a number of Scots, who probably didn't realise at the time that they would get further than any Scot would

---

[1] With special thanks to David Harding who provided some of these wonderful facts for a book we did for Japan/South Korea 2002.

ever achieve again, even in Ally's Army's wildest dreams. However, it was Uruguay and Argentina who each won their semi 6-1 and played a final in front of 90,000 in Montevideo. Argentinian fans were searched for guns on their way into the ground, giving the lie to the idea of security or hooliganism being recent/English respectively. 1-0 up, then 1-2 down by half-time, the Uruguayans bagged three second-half goals to become the inaugural winners of the Jules Rimet trophy. Uruguayans celebrated with a national holiday. Argentinians cheered themselves up by stoning the Uruguayan embassy across the water in Buenos Aires.

Uruguay maintained their unbeaten World Cup streak by chickening out in 1934 (**Italy**), with their striking players refusing to travel. It was left to Argentina, Brazil and the USA to represent the Americas, all losing their one and only game in an eight-team knockout structure. Egypt made it feel more like a world cup by becoming Africa's first representative. In the semi-finals, Italy – cheered on by rubbish dictator of the century, Benito Mussolini – beat Austria while Czechoslovakia beat Germany. Italy won the final 2-1.

* The final needed extra-time for the first time

* Average attendances were 23,235, which looks set to remain an all-time low

* Valdemar de Brito (Brazil) became the first player to miss a penalty in a world cup game

Uruguay's continued sulking saw them remain undefeated in 1938 (**France**), once again refusing to play. This left the door open to a second Italian win; also undefeated after three world cups, having not been at the first. This time the final saw another 4-2 victory, for Italy over the Hungarians.

- Argentina also refused to play; partly in consequence Cuba and the Dutch East Indies took part in what looks likely to be their only World Cup finals

- Sweden and Brazil contested a 3rd place play-off, also won 4-2 (by Brazil)

- Ernst Willimowski of Poland scored four goals in a game against Brazil

- Brazil nonetheless won the above match 6-5, with 11 goals still being a world cup aggregate record

With no World Cup in 1942 or 1946 Uruguay and Italy arrived in **Brazil** in 1950 still unbeaten in World Cups. Italy cracked first, losing 3-2 to Sweden. England appeared at a World Cup for the first time. India would have done, but FIFA refused to allow them to play in bare feet.[2] England and Scotland both made the final, providing between them the customary three officials of the day. With 13 teams in total, the group stage had a rather disorganised feel; one group was just a winner-takes-all play-off between Uruguay and Bolivia. Uruguay went 8-0 up and held on to win 8-0. The four group winners then contested another round robin; there was no final as such, although history presents it that way because the final match was between the best two teams: Brazil and Uruguay.

- Brazil had beaten Sweden (7-1) and Spain (6-1) and were overwhelming favourites against a Uruguay team who had beaten Sweden but only drawn against Spain

- This meant Brazil needed only a draw to top the group and claim the title

- 199,854 (give or take 146, although the crowd is also reported

---

[2] If this seems insane and trying to get a cheap laugh... it's not, it's true.

as 173,850) people watched expectantly as Brazil took the lead early in the second half

* 173,850 (give or take 26,150) then watched in disbelief as Uruguay stunned the home crowd to win 2-1; mass celebration in Uruguay, mass suicide in Brazil

* England, self-deluded masters of football, won their first game against Chile 2-0 with Stan Mortensen scoring England's first ever finals' goal

* They then lost 0-1 to the USA (famously reported in error as a 10-1 win by disbelieving journalists) and 0-1 to Spain

* Uruguayan Alcide Ghiggia became the first player to score in every game at a world cup; a feat repeated by Jairzinho of Brazil in 1970

In 1954 (**Switzerland**) some Germans (in the form of *West* Germany[3]) annoyed the footballing world for the first, but certainly not the last, time. Overwhelming favourites (in all senses) Hungary, with the Lionel Messi of his day Ferenc Puskás, was supposed to win. On their way to the final they indeed battered the Germans 8-3, though that did not eliminate Westgermany. They also beat the two 'finalists' from 1950, Brazil and Uruguay, to set up another game against the Germans in the final.

The Hungary-Brazil game became known as 'The Battle of Berne'. It saw a 4-2 Hungarian win, including three sending-offs by English

---

[3] It is an argument I have done to death elsewhere, that in 1954, 1974 and 1990 it was West Germany who won the World Cup, as well as losing it on other occasions like 1966. Entering two teams is fine (East and West), except you shouldn't then count those victories to the united version of the nation. Germany have thus won the world cup once only (in 2014), the same as England, and should get the excessive starage off those shirts. To further bolster my argument, I discover that a United Germany competed in the 1956, 1960 and 1964 Olympic Games. When allowed to enter only one team, the best they could manage was a single bronze medal.

referee Arthur Ellis – later one of the less notorious stars of TV's *It's a Knockout*. It was followed by a Brazilian invasion of the Hungarian dressing room. The injured Puskás proved useful even on the bench by threatening to bottle someone. Then came the final which was subsequently immortalised in German cinema as 'The Miracle of Berne', with the Germans coming from 0-2 down to win 3-2. How did the Germans beat the Mighty Magyars (unbeaten for four years and with a talisman who could juggle soap with his feet in the shower)? It seems it was a combination of an injured Puskás, the increasingly wet conditions and Adi Dassler's new screw-in studs used by the (West) Germans. And perhaps a touch of Magyar nerves. Anyway, the world collectively sighed 'well bugger me with a giant fish-fork' as *West* germany triumphed.

- Hungary's semi-final victory over Uruguay was Uruguay's first world cup defeat, 24 years after their first match

- Scotland made their first world cup finals, scoring none and conceding eight, a record they have rarely bettered

- England went out by the world cup's most popular score of the era: 4-2 in the quarter-finals to Uruguay. It is a record they have rarely bettered

- Sándor Kocsis of Hungary became the first player to score two hat-tricks in the same tournament, against South Korea and Westgermany

The world cup stayed in Europe in 1958; in **Sweden** to be precise. This is the beginning of the modern World Cup with some well-known features: four groups of four and Brazilian domination.

- The only World Cup with all four home nations in the finals, with Wales unlucky to lose to a single quarter-final goal by the tournament's youngest goal-scorer 'at 17 years and 239 days ' Pelé

- England got to the final. Well Englishman George Raynor did, as manager of the Swedes

- Juste Fontaine, Moroccan-born Frenchman banged in 13 tournament goals – still a record

The final was between Brazil and Sweden, who have played each other often in world cups; on this occasion, as so often on others, Brazil had the upper hand. The still 17-year-old Pelé bagged a brace in a 5-2 win. 1958 was probably Russia's best chance ever (as part of the USSR) of winning the World Cup, especially given that England were weakened by the Munich air disaster and that Russia had their own 'Pelé'.

The Extraordinary Tale of Eduard Streltsov: The Russian Pelé

Eduard Streltzov was a rebel, which wasn't a great thing to be in the 1950's Soviet Union. He was suspected of wanting to defect and, in a collective society, was in too much danger of becoming 'the story'. He wore sunglasses and a teddy boy quiff. He drank hard. He also offended important politicians. Accused of rape prior to the 1958 World Cup he was told by prosecutors that if he confessed he would be allowed to play in the finals. He confessed. The evidence against him was inconclusive and it is very much doubted that he received a fair trial, especially after being given that 'deal'. Subsequent to his death, chess player Anatoly Karpov has been amongst those campaigning for his posthumous acquittal, with the strong suspicion he was victimised by at least one member of the Politburo. He has come to adorn stamps and coins and his statue stands outside a stadium named after him.

His reputation is certainly more solid than the system and politicians who put him away.

In 1958, however, as Pelé was about to start his incredible career in the Swedish finals, Streltsov, subsequently nicknamed 'the Russian Pelé' and to back-heeling as Cryuff was to turning, was starting a 12-year sentence in the Stalinist state's gulag system. He dealt with the devil and got shafted. Initially beaten so badly by another prisoner that he spent four months in prison hospital, he was released after five years. Banned from professional football he began playing as an amateur for a factory team which started to do well and drew large crowds. When that cheeky chappy of Soviet era politics Leonid Brezhnev replaced Khrushchev as head of the Politburo he overturned the ban and Streltsov was able to play professionally for Torpedo Moscow again. He led them to the Russian title in his first season back; he then went on to play for the USSR again notching up more than creditable statistics, even if understandably not quite the force he was.

Clearly rape is a very serious matter and with books on Streltsov available only in Russian and Italian we are relying here on a rather good and lengthy Wikipedia piece which suggests that his guilt or otherwise is difficult to assess. Nonetheless, newspaper reports upon which the article is based, cast at least considerable doubt on the claims. Whatever the truth, Streltsov seems both a pawn and a victim of a flawed political system. As Mikhail Bakunin said, socialism without freedom is brutality and slavery. Although the obverse that freedom without socialism is privilege and injustice is also worth pointing out today. That last bit's not from Wikipedia; I saw it on a T-shirt. If Streltsov had been involved in 1958 and 1962 we might even talk of the USSR as former winners of the World Cup. His absence was a huge loss and if the system got him, it had also shot itself through the foot.

It would make a great film, wouldn't it? Especially if this is to be believed: he died 'in 1990 from throat cancer, which his first wife Alla later claimed had been brought about by irradiated food served to him in the camps. Seven years later, Marina Lebedeva, the woman Streltsov had confessed to raping, was seen laying flowers at his grave in Moscow on the day after the anniversary of his death.' https://en.wikipedia.org/wiki/Eduard_Streltsov (accessed 28/1/17).

If you doubt that he might have won the World Cup for the Soviet Union, he played for them in the Melbourne Olympic Games of 1956. In the semi-final against Bulgaria he is generally believed to have dragged his team to the final, from being 1-0 down with two players injured in extra-time. One of those injured was Torpedo's Ivanov, and Streltsov lost his place in the final because the coach believed in playing two strikers from the same club side.[4] His replacement in the final offered Streltsov his gold medal, which he refused on the grounds that he would go on to win much else. He had reason to be cocky - though perhaps he became too cocky - but it is one of football's greatest 'what ifs'. Rules changed such that squad members also got medals, but by the time this happened in 2006 he was too dead to receive it.

In 1962 the tournament returned to South America with 57 teams attempting to be one of 14 qualifiers to join hosts **Chile** and holders Brazil. The tournament is most remembered for a number of extremely hostile encounters, including most notably Chile v Italy, which became known as the *Battle of Santiago*. As well as the two sending-offs and a broken nose, there was also much spitting from the Chileans and occasional sniper fire from the stands.[5]

---

[4] Oh for the days when any manager believed in playing two strikers in the first place!

[5] This is all true apart from the last bit.

Like the *Battle of Berne*, the one in Santiago was refereed by an Englishman, Kenneth Aston.

- Colombia and Bulgaria qualified for the first time
- Vaclav Masek of Czechoslovakia scored after just 16 seconds against Mexico, the quickest ever World Cup goal
- Chile spat their way to a third-place finish
- After the Valdivia earthquake of 1960 (the most powerful ever recorded at about 9.5 on the Richter scale), the tournament had to be hastily rescheduled with several venues becoming unavailable
- The semi-final between Brazil and Chile was also re-located from Viña del Mar to the capital after the hosts' surprise qualification; this annoyed a fair number of Chileans in the originally scheduled location. Brazil won the match by the world cup's favourite scoreline of 4-2

Brazil drew 0-0 with Czechoslovakia in the group stages and faced them again in the final. This time both teams scored in the opening 20 minutes, with Brazil quickly cancelling out a Czechoslovak lead. Brazil scored twice in the second half to retain the cup 3-1.

The score-line 4-2 was still determined to have a say in 1966, this time after extra-time on July 30th in **England.** Since you probably know the story well, here are some key features:

- The world cup was stolen and then found by Pickles (a dog)[6]
- Wingless wonders
- Injured Jimmy Greaves replaced by hat-trick hero Geoff Hurst

---

[6] I realise that sentence may be ambiguous; to be clear: Pickles did not steal the trophy, he only found it later.

- People on the pitch thinking it was all over in extra time

- Bobby Moore

- Small boys in the park, jumpers for goal-posts etc.

- North Koreans beating Italians

It would take Germany nearly 50 years before they finally won their first world cup in 2014, although *West*germany would, admittedly, take the title again in 1974 and 1990.

The Quite Extraordinary (but not as extraordinary as the tale of Eduard Streltsov) Tale of Lev Yashin

Like Streltsov, Lev Yashin won Olympic gold with the USSR in 1956, possibly, of course, because of the Hungarian refusal to play over the smallest of fraternal invasions. Like Steltsov he has a statue at Luzhniki, is credited with revolutionising the way football was played and failed to outlive the Soviet Union. If Streltsov had to wait for his gold medal until after his death, Yashin was already dead a decade when FIFA declared him the best goalkeeper of the 20th Century.

Yashin was born into a family of workers in 1929, although that was pretty much compulsory at the time, and went to work in a factory aged thirteen. Ditto. He is believed to have done two things excessively: trained and smoked. He was the pioneer of the thrown clearance, as well as leaving the area to support the defence, and developed into a tremendous keeper known for both shot-stopping (around 150 penalties) and taking crosses. Because of his distinctive black garb he was known as the 'black spider', the 'black octopus' and, despite its limbular limitations, the 'black panther'.

Yashin played in three consecutive global tournaments, as well as helping the USSR to the European crown of 1960. If the Soviets might have won the World Cup in 1958 before sending their best player to a labour camp, they also had a chance in 1966. Based for the group stages in the grim, industrial north east (presumably to make them feel at home) they romped through the group games, beating the Italians along the way. Yashin conceded a solitary goal. For the quarter-finals they remained at Roker Park and beat the Hungarians, with whom they were now jolly good comradely chums again.

The move away from the north east to the southern paradise of Liverpool didn't go well for totalitarian workers' utopias. North Korea took out the Italians at Ayresome Park, Middlesbrough, but then lost at Goodison to Portugal in the quarter-final, despite taking a 3-0 lead. The USSR's move to Goodison also saw them founder at the hands of Westgermany despite Yashin's best efforts. Then they lost the third-place play-off at Wembley, though the land of the tractor factory had the last laugh as a 'Russian' (Soviet) linesman saw what the crowd wanted him to see in the final.

As for Yashin, the excessive smoking led to gangrene and a leg amputation in 1984. He died six years later in 1990, the same year as Streltsov.]

In **Mexico**, 1970, we saw the first non-South American or European World Cup. It was now in the familiar 'four groups of four following qualification' format. Beautiful football by Brazil (including that lovely team move and thwack of a finish by Carlos Alberto – lots of passes and some side-stepping in midfield reminiscent of Phil

Bennett for the Barbarians[7]) and a 4-1 thrashing of Italy in the final; as three-time winners, Brazil got to keep the Jules Rimet Trophy. It was stolen, and lost forever, 10 years later however, and Pickles was no longer on the scene by then.

Brazil had qualified in the same group as England, beating them 1-0. It was the match which saw *that* save by Gordon Banks.[8] Defending Champions England went on to a quarter-final against the Germany West team, squandering a 2-0 lead and learning the 'never write them off' lesson the hard way, defeated 3-2. The semi-final between Italy and Westgermany was a remarkable game which went to type. First the Italians scored early and clung on to a 1-0 lead. Later the West Germans scored late: a 90th minute equaliser. In extra-time, the Germans took the lead before Italy equalised and regained the lead themselves. Germany equalised again before Italy finally won 4-3. The suggestion was made that the extra-time affected the Italian performance in the final, although it didn't stop the Westies winning the 3rd-place play-off the day before.

- Lesser known qualifiers this time were Israel and El Salvador. The former got creditable draws against Sweden and Italy. The latter's record of scored nil conceded nine in three defeats may not seem in any way creditable but is actually better than they managed in a single match of the 1982 finals

- Anatoli Pusatch of the USSR became the first substitute to be used in the world cup finals

- The Italy v Germany semi-final, the Germany v Uruguay

---

[7] Here's that goal: https://www.youtube.com/watch?v=M5HbmeNKino Accessed 12/10/2016 and if you're too young to know what Phil Bennett jinking is, take this, accessed minutes later: https://www.youtube.com/watch?v=AwCbG4I0QyA Egg-chasing it might be but sensational nonetheless.

[8] Still gives me goosebumps and I was only four at the time: https://www.youtube.com/watch?v=HNLam4RAbg8 Accessed 12/10/2016.

3rd-place play-off and the Brazil v Italy final were all played at Mexico City's Azteca Stadium and all attracted crowds in excess of 100,000

- *East*germany made the final in the form of referee and Trabant salesman Rudi Glöckner[9]

- The best young player award went to Cubillas of Peru; it is a name which haunts Scots of a certain age to this very day

Western Germany, 1974. Twenty years after ruining everyone's world cup by hoofing the free-flowing Magyars off the park thanks to screw-in studs, the Westgermans were at it again, this time defeating The Netherlands' total football (Cruyff, Neeskens and all) in the final despite an English referee giving the Dutch a very early penalty. Scotland, but not England, qualified this time and I watched, frustrated, with David Jenkinson who soon after moved to Helensburgh, Dumbartonshire – just one of those things that sticks even though I was eight. Scotland actually drew with Yugoslavia (thanks to a late Joe Jordan equaliser) and Brazil (0-0) as well as beating Zaire. But since Yugoslavia and Brazil also drew, qualification was decided by margin of victory versus Zaire. Yugoslavia +9, Brazil +3, Scotland +2. Scotland were out, rather unluckily.

- Carlos Caszely of Chile was sent off by red card in a World Cup match, the first player so dismissed

- Scotland were the first team eliminated from the world cup finals without losing a match

- As well as Zaire, Haiti were also playing in their first world cup; neither impoverished nation did much to raise spirits

---

[9] This is just one of a number of 'facts' that I've made up to make it more interesting, although if someone will add it to Wikipedia it will become fact in due course.

back home, although Haiti were winning their opening match against Italy for six minutes before losing 3-1. Sadly, next up was a 0-7 loss to Poland

- Westgermany became the second team to lose at the group stage but win the trophy; they were also the first team to do this in 1954

Germany played with itself at the group stage. Westgermany v Eastgermany, with the latter famously winning, though with both teams progressing. Wikipedia offers the opinion that 'this embarrassing result forced a realignment of the West German team that helped them win the Cup' which simply boosts my argument that entering two teams is cheating and that those stars *really* need to be removed from today's German shirts; they can have one star – like us and Spain and France.

And if you will now permit me to get out my enormous crowbar, in her book *Lost in Static*, Christina Philippou uses the highly effective/ amusing idea of someone looking or feeling as uncomfortable as Lucas Radebe (Kaiser Chiefs,[10] Leeds United and South Africa) in a tutu. This Zairean defender (Illungu, I think) of a Brazilian free-kick seems to me to qualify for this description: https://www.youtube. com/watch?v=aYDXkVGpMpc (Accessed 12/10/2016)

Scotland were going to win in **Argentina** in 1978. We're on the march with Ally's army indeed![11] Given the strength of the team, this is not such an absurd statement, but after the disappointing manner of exit from 1974's tournament, Scotland were able to go one better (or worse). First up they lost to Cubillas' Peru with one

---

[10] NOT the band

[11] 1978 saw the claim north of the border that 'we'll really shake 'em up when we win the world cup, cos Scotland are the greatest football team'. It's scary how not totally ridiculous that seemed at the time as they beat eventual runners-up Holland.

of those free-kicks which is so inventive it's hardly ever done again; a bit like the left-footed drive Roberto Carlos got right once in a thousand times, but much more of a stabby, toe-poke with the outside of the right boot. Jay-Jay did something similar for Bolton once. I think it probably says something about British (I mean British) football arrogance at that time that this was seen as an appalling loss. But in all honesty, and despite my track record of 'tartan-teasing', was it? It was in South America during the golden age of Peruvian football. After the 1970 World Cup, when Peru exited at the same stage as the World Champions, England, Pelé himself anointed Cubillas as his successor as best footballer in the world. Although not qualifying for Westgermany 1974, Peru did win the Copa América a year later, beating Brazil 3-1 (in Brazil) on the way. By 1978, Cubillas (the Pelé of Peru) should not have been a shock. But he was and it knocked the stuffing out of the Scots.

Scotland could then only draw against pre-Ayatollah Iran, which, combined with a comfortable win by Peru against the same team, meant that Scotland needed to win by three clear goals against Holland to qualify. In modern terms, Scotland 'bossed it completely', and were unlucky to go behind to a very soft penalty. However, equalizing on the stroke of half-time – which they fully deserved – they moved into a 3-1 lead including Archie Gemmill's brilliant solo effort.[12] This put Scotland 'in dream land', as David Coleman observed. Indeed! They fell asleep and conceded a second to a Johnny Rep strike which the 'monstrously permed, part-time goal-keeper' Alan Rough (so described in the Amazon blurb to MacColl's book (2008)) could not be held responsible for.

If Scotland's eternal duel with England for the most painful exit/ non-qualification was seeing its opening salvoes, Holland were even more painfully finding another host nation to lose to. This time Argentina, then ruled by a murderous *Junta* which made

---

[12] https://www.youtube.com/watch?v=eyJTBrbPIHQ (Accessed 18/10/2016)

the staging of the finals there controversial in the first place. *En route* Argentina needed to beat Peru by four clear goals to avoid elimination and to qualify at the expense of arch-rivals Brazil. In the end they managed just six in a staggeringly easy match. Cubillas, interviewed on the subject, offers no hint of anything 'fishy', although haddock-flavoured clue number one is that Peru did field a goalkeeper born in Argentina. Even fishier ('Argies are cheating bastards who wouldn't have done better than England without cheating', screams The Sun), it is worth noting this from 2012:

> Former Peruvian Senator Genaro Ledesma has confirmed the shock result was agreed before the match by the dictatorships of the two countries. Mr Ledesma, 80, made the accusations to Buenos Aires judge Noberto Oyarbide, who last week issued an order of arrest against former Peruvian military president Francisco Bermúdez. He is accused of illegally sending 13 Peruvian citizens to Argentina as part of the so-called Condor Plan, through which Latin American dictatorships in the 1970s cooperated in the repression of political dissidents.

> Once inside Argentina, the prisoners were tortured by the brutal military regime and forced to sign false confessions. Mr Ledesma, an opposition leader at the time, claims Argentinian dictator Jorge Videla only accepted the political prisoners on condition that Peru deliberately lost the World Cup match – and by enough goals to ensure Argentina progressed. He said in court: 'Videla needed to win the World Cup to cleanse Argentina's bad image around the world. So he only accepted the group [of political prisoners] if Peru allowed the Argentine national team to triumph.'[13]

---

[13] Read more: http://www.dailymail.co.uk/sport/football/article-2098970/ Argentina-cheated-World-Cup-1978-says-Peru-senator.html#ixzz4NWb7J5wH (Accessed 18/10/2016)

Once the world-cup-winning factor had faded, the Junta later went on to save Margaret Thatcher's political career by sending hundreds of young men to unnecessarily bleak deaths in The Falklands. Not really football, you're right. Anyway, Peru had already been eliminated before that match and surely some bright spark would work out eventually that final matches needed to be played at the same time to at least minimise this type of thing? Brazil were eliminated on goal difference. Argentina went on to win in one of the most tainted tournaments ever. Reporters on the cup were advised to learn handy phrases like 'please don't torture me' and 'please deliver my body to my family'. Let us just remember the jinking Gemmill goal and forget the rest, eh?

But no! Amazingly no one *had* realized that the last group matches should be played simultaneously. And so in **Spain, 1982** we were treated to *The Disgrace of Gijón* (whose team is ironically called 'Sporting'). A single goal win for Westgermany in the group's final match would see the Germans and Austrians qualify at the expense of Algeria, who had shocked everyone with an opening game win against Westgermany. The Germans duly took the lead after 10 minutes and thereafter kicked the ball back and forth with neither team making a serious attempt to score. In Germany this is known as a 'non-aggression pact' and was a perfect storm of bargaining positions with both teams qualifying, but Austria prepared to accept defeat given an easier-looking route forward. It does appear here that it was the 'system' at fault, with both sets of players working out that passivity would lead to outcomes acceptable to both parties, rather than planned collusion. However, elsewhere the non-spectacle has been known as 'the deceit' or even *Anschluss*, referring to the 1938 joining of the two countries with rather more serious results.

And Westgermany's villainy wasn't over (is it *ever?*), as the tournament is most remembered, apart from Gerry Armstrong scoring the winner for Northern Ireland against hosts Spain, for

Harald Schumacher attempting to decapitate Patrick Battiston in their semi-final penalty triumph against France. He was not sent off. Fortunately for truth,justice and fairness in football, Paolo Rossi scored a hat-trick in the final, which Italy won 3-1 against the Germans; he had recently returned to football after a bribery scandal.

If FIFA had finally worked out that final group matches needed to be played simultaneously by **Mexico 1986**, some other things hadn't changed. In this case, Argentina's determination to cheat their way through tournaments; specifically Maradona's hand of God incident. Actually, I managed to shout 'hand ball' on a portable black and white TV after half a bottle of orange brandy, so what was the referee thinking? Anyway, apologies for going all 'Daily Mail' on you, but if you discount the times Argentina cheated and the times Westgermany won rather than Germany, England has won the World Cup as often as Germany and Argentina combined.[14] Hooray! Anyway, Argentina beat the Westgermans 3-2 in the final with Marcelo Trobbiani coming on for the last two minutes. Trobbiani had been a strange inclusion in the squad with manager Carlos Bilardo making it clear he was unlikely to play, but rather he would be used in tactical training matches. He played the role so tirelessly that he was given the last two minutes of the final, managing a single back-heel touch of the ball before picking up a winners' medal.

It is difficult to look back on **Italy, 1990** without weeping pitifully. England's best world cup outside England ended in

---

[14] I should counter-balance this jingoistic nonsense by mentioning that at the time of writing there has just been in the news the tale of a piece of post-Brexit bragging; a hoodie for sale with a Union Jack coloured in map of the UK and underneath it is intended to say 'We're number 1''. Except it actually says 'Were #1'. Amazing how many bigots can't write, spell, use apostrophes etc. – that's given me every incentive to proofread this properly at least!!! In the general election of 2017, UKIP believed in 'intergration not immigration' as another, for instance.

cruel fashion, but the tournament had started so promisingly. Nine-man Cameroon had one player sent off for nothing, then another who was guilty of attempted murder, but still ran out 1-0 winners against world champions Argentina. The attempted murder has particular comedy value as Caniggia runs down the pitch for Argentina like a 110-metre hurdler, jumping one tackle after another until he finally gets flattened. The would-be assassin loses his boot in a tackle Roy Keane would have been proud of, and if you're watching the clip, you should look out for the crafty Argentinian stamp on his be-socked foot. With you all the way, Alf! In their next match Maradona's penchant for basketball is given a further outing with a fine right-handed save.

Nowadays it has become unfashionable in England to mock teams for not qualifying ahead of Costa Rica, but in 1990 it was all the rage as Scotland's 1-0 defeat to the Central Americans made their win against Sweden and narrow defeat to Brazil irrelevant. Another painful exit. A painful stay, on the other hand, was offered up by Jack Charlton's Republic of Ireland who, through a hybrid of Gaelic football, hurling, rugby union and hypnosis, bored their way further through a tournament than any team has before. I know it's traditional to emphasise their 'pluck', the great support, the 'craic' etc. – and good luck to 'em – but do not kid yourself that they were anything other than dull and lucky (and mostly cockney). The world cup equivalent of the Championship side which finishes 6th and then wins the play-offs. They only bothered to score when they were behind, and there's only so often you can pull that trick off, with their luck running out versus Italy in the quarter-finals after beating Romania on penalties in the last 16. Thank you, Toto!

Much more interesting were a) René Higuita who entertainingly knocked his Colombian team out with bizarre goalkeeping, b) players I'd forgotten about, like Yugoslavia's Stoichkov and Belgium's Enzo Scifo and c) England, who were in the business of last-minute volleys (from soon to be balding horse David Platt)[15] against Belgium and a come-from-behind win against Cameroon. Both those wins after extra time. In fact, none of England's performances suggested they could be world beaters, apart from the game in which they got beaten, oddly enough. That was, of course, semi-final defeat to (still) Westgermany on penalties; Gazza cried, Pavarotti sang, we all cried. If you want to claim some sort of victory, compare the world cup songs of the respective countries – you can't say the Westgermans didn't have a sense of humour after that ditty.

So the final was cheat v cheat. Maradona v Klinnsman. I was so distraught I couldn't watch. And if you think 'Klinsy' improved his image in the Premier League you should see the penalty he won in the quarter-finals v Czechoslovakia. Double twist. Pike. Everything. And then he got someone sent off in the final by pretending that he'd been AK47ed (if that is now an acceptable verb). It's only with the writing of this book that I've been able to bring myself to watch the highlights of that match, which appears to have provided one of the most inept and overly dramatic refereeing performances of all time. At a remove of 28 years, I even have some sympathy with the Argentinian players. Well, a little, possibly, though not Maradona, obviously. And if you want to claim another odd victory, Gazza's crying was much, much more heart-rending and sincere than cheating Diego's.

- The total rubbishness of this world cup probably led to changes in the back-pass law of 1992, which explains the upsurge of interest in the Premier League more than SKY popping Curiosity Killed the Cat on a podium and tittering creepily at cheerleaders

---

[15] The anti-Anglo conspiracy theory, however, is given credence by the goal John Barnes had disallowed; I mean he was only a yard onside! YouTube it; freeze-frame it if you don't believe me.

- Argentina in a victory for total(ly rubbish) football managed to be runners-up with almost as many red cards (3) as goals (5).

The most pleasing thing about **USA 1994** was that US capitalism produced a good deal of England merch, only to find out that England had failed to qualify. Such was the level of football knowledge in the USA at the time, that many ordinary punters who filled the sports bars to watch basketball and baseball, thought that a US victory over England in a mini-warm up tournament was what had eliminated the English. Brazil won the final against... Italy, I think, but in another utterly forgettable finals here are your official highlights:

- Diego Maradona was sent home for taking drugs (Cheating? Surely not?!)
- Roger Milla, who must've been 80 in the 1990 world cup, scored again for Cameroon in these finals aged 84ish.
- Despite the USA not having a Major Soccer League (like it does now) average attendances at these finals approached 70,000 – presumably people from other countries who now lived in the States and were desperate to see some proper sport

The low light was what happened to poor old Andrés Escobar. He scored an own goal in Colombia's defeat by the USA and was promptly murdered on returning home. And Beckham thought he was made a scapegoat four years on

Four years on was **France 1998**. Most remembered in England for what happened to England, of course, which in case you don't remember was a) a pre-pubescent Michael Owen scoring a wonder-goal against Argentina, b) cheating (still) Diego Simeone completely over-reacting and getting David Beckham sent off, although Beckham learned a lot, c) Sol Campbell scoring a perfectly good golden goal in extra time which the over-fussy referee disallowed, d) Argentina winning on penalties, e) David Beckham being indeed made the scapegoat, but nobody shot him.

Although not always at their brightest throughout the tournament, the French did what they do best. I mean the fans, not the team; they gradually got behind a winning project (although always ready to boo at any moment). No booing was necessary in the final, however, as a less than fluid progress to the final brought France up against an even less fluid Brazil team and a rather easy 3-0 win. In other news:

- Barry Davies (I think) opined that Croatia played with the freedom of a team without a history; nice to see someone commentating with the freedom of a man without an education

- Croatia did impressively finish third with Robert Prosinecki scoring along the way, having previously done so for Yugoslavia

2002 **Japan/South Korea** was the last time I wrote a book about the World Cup. It was also the last time golden goals were used in the World Cup. It was the first time the World Cup had been held outside of Europe or the Americas and therefore the first time in Asia. It got off to a cracking start with Senegal beating holders France in the first game. If memory serves, France were eliminated without scoring a goal and second favourites Argentina also fell at the first hurdle thanks to England and also Anders Svensson. Senegal lost in the quarter-final to another surprise package, Turkey. England found themselves in the very hard half of the draw and went out in the quarters to stand-out team Brazil. Unfortunate perhaps, but mercifully without penalties, disallowed goals in extra-time etc. Just a straightforward defeat, against ten men. In the other half of the draw (the easy half) Germany plotted a route past the 2nd Camberley Apache Cub Scouts and then the Dog and Duck (Macclesfield) Reserves, got to the final easily and then lost to Brazil.

In all, well, something approaching seriousness, England got two draws and a win against highly-rated Argentina to reach the knockout phase. They then demolished Denmark (3-0) and narrowly lost to eventual winners Brazil. It is the kind of World Cup we can only dream of now! Germany meanwhile sneaked past Paraguay, the USA and South Korea all by the single goal of the game and got nowhere near Brazil.

- After the first World Cup took place in Uruguay (defending Olympic champions) in 1930, Japan were, effectively, only the second team to host the competition without having previously played in it. The first was Italy 1934. The third will (for some unbeknownst reason) be Qatar in 2022.

Germany (fully unified and never having won the World Cup) were extremely lucky to host the 2006 version. At least so say the conspiracy theorists who cite arms embargoes lifted against Saudi Arabia, mysterious voting abstentions, investments in Thailand etc. etc. in the build-up. However, South Africa got it next time anyway and I think it is about time we realized how unlikely it is that FIFA would ever be involved in any kind of corruption. Besides, I haven't got the time to substantiate any of the allegations I'm not making.

Hosts Germany were at an all-time low FIFA ranking of 22 just months before the tournament and barely sneaked into the top 20 by the time it started. To give you an idea, 22 is below where Iceland stand as I write and, let's face it, they're hopeless. Even so, with much flag-waving which had been discouraged for the previous 60 years, the Germans managed 3rd place and the tournament as a whole was considered a great success. After the craziness of 2002, six of the quarter-finalists in Germany were former winners. Germany won on penalties. England lost on them. As before, England went out without really losing – at least more recently they've spared us that by just losing in normal time.

The final will be remembered not so much for Zidane and Materazzi scoring the goals (1-1 after extra-time) but for their *contretemps* which finished with Zidane head-butting the Italian in the chest and thereby getting sent off. Whether his consequent exclusion from the penalty shoot-out was decisive we'll never know, but France lost it. Many rumours abound about what was said by Materazzi to provoke the assault, with a host of lip-readers wading in to declare that it was about 'terrorism', 'sisters and mothers' etc. and deciding whether it was or wasn't racist. Frankly, I find by far and away the least convincing argument that Materazzi opined that ciabatta and salami was in all respects a better mid-afternoon snack than baguette and brie.

- Graham Poll became the first world cup referee to book a player three times in a single match before finally sending off the offending Croatian v Australia. Those of us who saw his monstrous ego ruin Bishop's Stortford matches many seasons previously were not surprised

In 2010 Paul the Octopus correctly predicted the result of the final by eating a mussel from a box with the Spanish flag on it. Apparently. The tournament itself was held in **South Africa** and I think tells you a lot about why not everyone gets football. Spain dominated the player of the tournament 'dream team' vote despite getting off to a losing start against the Swiss; but once past the group stages, Spain's progress was as follows:

Last 16: Beat Portugal 1-0 with a second-half goal

Quarter-Final: Beat Paraguay 1-0 with a second-half goal

Semi-Final: Beat Germany 1-0 with a second-half goal

Final: Beat Holland 1-0 with a goal in the second half, of extra time.

The team with all the talent, the apparent crème de la crème, was impersonating Liverpool circa 1985.

By these finals it is impossible to discuss the tournament without, at least, nodding at bribery and corruption allegations. Should these finals really have gone to Morocco? Possibly.

- Most notable for Paul the predictive squid and Sepp Blatter apologizing; in this case to England and Mexico for terrible refereeing decisions which probably had no bearing on the result

- Some England fans voiced their frustration at England's performance leading to criticism from Wayne Rooney; never mind that he earned in a day about the same as some of those people had been saving up for years to be able to afford to go and watch

You possibly remember **Brazil** 2014? A united Germany finally got the right to wear one lone star on its shirt by beating Argentina 1-0 in the final. Their semi-final against the hosts is possibly one of the most extraordinary games in World Cup history. Although Brazil had not overly impressed, they were at home and have won the thing five times. A close contest was expected. However, just as Uruguay's 1950 triumph shocked everyone, Germany's demolition of the hosts took everyone by surprise. Frankly it could have been more, but a late consolation for Brazil failed to add any respectability to proceedings as it finished 1-7.

Three-time losing finalists Holland had possibly the most frustrating tournament, running into a lack of form at just the wrong time. Having opened up with a 5-1 thrashing of the holders Spain they won their other group matches. However in the last 16 they stuttered, although ultimately found a way of breaking the *corazón* of every Mexican with two very late goals to win 2-1. In the quarter-finals, only penalties saw them beat Costa Rica after a 0-0 draw, and in the semi-finals the tables were turned as they this time lost on penalties to Argentina after another goalless affair. Deprived of the chance to win their first world cup against the *oude* enemy, they then found their scoring boots again, dispatching the psychologically frazzled Brazilians 0-3 for third place. The less said about England the better, although they didn't lose to Costa Rica, did they?

And so the fun will all start again in Russia in 2018. Next up: Who got there and how.

References/Reading

MacColl, G. (2008), 78: *How a Nation Lost the World Cup*, Headline Books

Philippou, C (2016), *Lost in Static*, Urbane Books

The Road to Russia: Qualification

209 teams from six confederations started out on the road, with a format which allows for the odd surprise but little genuine giant-killing. As well as the hosts Russia, thirteen European teams qualified from nine groups; nine winners and four from play-offs between the eight best runners-up. Then there are five group winners from Africa, after a whittling-down process to get to those groups. The top four qualify from South America's ten-team 'super-group'. Asia whittles down to two groups from which the top two qualify, making four. And CONCACAF also whittles before three qualify from a six-team hexagonal/final group. That makes 30 teams.

In Asia, the 3rd-placed teams in the final groups play-off for the right to play-off against the 4th-placed team in CONCACAF's hexagon for one of the remaining two places. The 5th-placed South American team also gets a play-off against the winners of Oceania. Oceania don't get an automatic place for a variety of reasons, most notably because they are often proud warrior nations who prefer rugby. That and the fact that they're not very good at football. New Zealand play in Oceania as do Papua New Guinea. In the odd world of sport Australia has been moved to Asia and Israel has been moved to Europe, but for rather different reasons.

The qualification processes give an advantage to higher-ranked teams, with byes through early rounds (where applicable) and plenty of time for recovery in home and away group stages. But when things had all settled there were still one or two surprises and new faces getting ready for Russia.

Europe

There weren't too many surprises in Europe early doors, but given that Panama looked like they might qualify from CONCACAF the bias towards European teams didn't seem excessive. For instance in Group A France, Netherlands *and* Sweden were all involved and one would miss out even on a play-off. Meanwhile in Group G only Spain or Italy – both recent winners - would qualify automatically. Possibly the biggest shock early in the piece came in Group C where Germany were well clear. No, of course that wasn't the shock – rather that in the race for a play-off slot Northern Ireland and Azerbaijan led Czechia, a footballing nation well and truly in the doldrums. Group I saw four pretty good teams separated by just two points with four to play, Croatia and Iceland (13) just heading Turkey and Ukraine (11), with all those teams having lost only once. Two games later and they'd all lost twice with Croatia/Iceland (16) heading Turkey/Ukraine (14).

If it was going to be close in Group I, it wasn't remotely tense in Group C. The penultimate matches saw Germany qualify on the same night as England, with a 1-3 victory in Northern Ireland, putting the Germans eight points clear. Meanwhile, Czechia's 1-2 win in Azerbaijan closed the gap on Northern Ireland to just 7 points with a game to play. In Group E Christian Eriksen's 16th-minute goal for Denmark away to Montenegro in the penultimate match was crucial, with both teams having been on the same points before the game, seeking to take the play-off spot behind the Poles.

Ultimately, Europe provided shocks of sorts all round. If the final table for Group A looks close, it wasn't. Netherlands didn't have such a bad campaign but ended up needing to beat Sweden 7-0 in their final game to pip them to the play-offs. They only managed two. Had they reversed their 0-1 defeat at home to group winners France, the Dutch would actually have won the group. Fine margins. In Group B the Swiss won their first nine qualifying games but had to settle for the play-offs having lost in Lisbon. Not only did Valente Silva score the crucial second in a 2-0 win, he also became known as the 'unbookable one'; I mean he didn't look related to the referee? But if that is the way Silva plays normally he has to be worth a bet on being sent off in Russia. Northern Ireland claimed the play-off spot from Group C and the Republic of Ireland managed the same in Group D; the former a surprise on historical record, the second on needing to win away to a Welsh side having a superb unbeaten run. I think I'm right in saying that had Wales drawn they would have a) completed the qualifying campaign undefeated b) still not made the play-offs being the second-placed team with the worst record. So don't feel too agonised in the valleys. Once again superb singing of the anthem, though. Poland qualified ahead of Denmark in Group E. Lewandowski scored lots. That wasn't a shock.

The shock in Group F was that the battle to finish behind England was ultimately pointless. Slovakia would have qualified if they'd not conceded a last-minute winner in their penultimate match against Scotland – an own goal by Liverpool's best central defender Skrtel. And Scotland would have qualified if they'd managed a last-minute winner in their last match against Slovakia. However with Slovakia edging Scotland on goal difference in the group, they were still the second-placed team with the worst record and it was

Eire who benefited from all this. In Group G improving Albania really had no chance, finishing third behind winners Spain and runners-up Italy who would have to take their play-off chances with the likes of Greece who were runners-up in Group H to Belgium. The major shock here was that Belgium didn't win all ten matches, drawing at home to the Greeks. And hats off to Iceland in Group I. Proving that their first major tournament in Euro 2016 was no fluke, they made their first World Cup, the only country of fewer than a million people to do so. Ever. They won seven of 10 games against decent teams like Croatia (2nd), Ukraine and Turkey and were the group's top scorers. I have, however, had to stop following the Reykjavík Grapevine twitter account after levels of smugness and gloating got unbearable.

And all that left just four places still open via the play-offs. When the draw was made ... this is what it revealed.

Northern Ireland v Switzerland

Corry Evans got hit on the back and a penalty was awarded by the Romanian referee. Corry Evans' wife got all abusive/racist on twitter as a result. She later apologised, but it just felt like it wasn't going to happen for the team I had once mocked as NINIL (Northern Ireland Nil). The second leg finished 0-0 and Switzerland went though. (Aggregate: Switzerland 1-0 NINIL)

Denmark v Republic of Ireland

Having drawn the away leg 0-0 and taken an early lead in the home match, Eire probably thought they had done the hard part. Well actually the hard part will be working out how they were losing by half-time and in the end conceded five. (Aggregate: Denmark 5-1 Republic of Ireland)

Croatia v Greece

Greece almost did the impossible. No I don't mean almost qualifying for the World Cup after losing twice to the Faroe Islands in Euro-qualification two years previously. I mean making Dejan Lovren look like an accomplished defender. In a display which made Garry Birtles sound like he needed a lamppost to smash his head against, Greece were demolished 4-1 away and then managed just eight shots at home in a 0-0 formality. (Aggregate: Croatia 4-1 Greece)

Sweden v Italy

Presumably Italian design was upon 0-0 away and sneaking a 1-0 at home. However it was the Swedes who travelled to Italy with a 1-0 lead. The 0-0 draw in the second leg was therefore enough for them to make light of their tough draw and ensure Italy would not be at the World Cup for the first time in 60 years. In a group with Spain they may have been unlucky, but in not scoring at home (making four nil-nil draws in eight European play-off matches) they had only themselves to blame in the end.

Africa

Looking at things from as far back as 2016 it seemed entirely possible that the qualification process might give us the usual suspects: Tunisia, Nigeria, Ivory Coast, Senegal and Egypt. At the same time, Burkina Faso and Uganda had put in some solid performances in early qualification, along with the Cape Verde Islands, who at the time of the World Cup draw were *still* ranked by FIFA above Russia.

In Group A Tunisia did pip DR Congo by virtue of the Congolese side's only defeat; away in Tunisia 2-1. However, equally significant was the game in Kinshasa which the home team led comfortably 2-0 with just 15 minutes left. However, two goals in a minute saw the Tunisians escape with a point. They finished just a point ahead of DRC and qualified.

In Group B Nigeria romped home. There was much more last-day drama in Abidjan (Group C) where the Ivory Coast were at home knowing that victory against Morocco would send them to the finals. However, two first-half goals for the away team dampened the enthusiasm of the home crowd, and a 0-2 win was enough to send Morocco back to the finals for the first time this century. Les Éléphants of Côte D'Ivoire would have scored lots of points in Gaelic football as they were very good at booting it over the bar all game.

In Group D Senegal led the way, even if both Burkina Faso and the Cape Verde Islands did manage to leave South Africa bottom of the group. And finally in Group E Uganda did well to push Egypt, but in the end suffered for their inability to score goals. Just three goals for and two against in six matches.

South America

Two thirds into the qualification process and Argentina were 5th, facing the prospect of a play-off to qualify. If the notion of a play-off against Oceania winners might seem easy enough, they headed Colombia in 6th by only a single point thanks largely to having beaten the boys from Bogotá twice. Both Brazil and Argentina have flirted with non-qualification in the past but the results are usually predictable. Those two qualify usually joined by Uruguay, Chile, Colombia; less often by Ecuador, Paraguay, Peru; hardly ever by Bolivia and never by Venezuela, whose tastes are traditionally more North American, i.e. baseball.

Shortly before the last round of matches I read an article about whether Maradona or Messi would be regarded as Argentina's greatest. The argument seemed to be that Maradona would be declared the winner if Argentina were knocked out of the World Cup before the finals for the first time since 1970. And it didn't look good as they needed to win away in Ecuador and had not done so in the altitude of Quito since the start of the century. Argentina do have a high-altitude training camp in their own northern provinces but even so their trips to Bolivia and Ecuador are always tricky. I witnessed them lose a tempestuous affair in La Paz in 1997. And this time they were 1-0 down inside a minute. Alas though, this story does not have a happy ending. Argentina's poor qualifying campaign – and the little man's reputation - was salvaged by a Messi hat-trick, allowing them to qualify in third behind Brazil and Uruguay.

That left the final qualifying place and a play-off place still to play for. Colombia would have had to have results go against them dramatically to miss out altogether. Leading 0-1 in Lima in the final few minutes they looked comfortable. Meanwhile Chile, who started the campaign inflicting Brazil's only qualifying defeat, had lost control of their destiny; 3-0 down in São Paulo they needed a Colombian victory to clinch the play-off spot. However, Peru equalised against Colombia. The latter qualified 4th instead of 3rd, but the former snatched the play-off match-up against New Zealand on goal difference. Despite being the only team ranked in FIFA's top ten not to make the finals, Chile were not the major surprise casualty of the night (which happened in CONCACAF) but it did mean that both Alexis Sánchez and Virgil Van Dijk would not be playing in Russia, something not even a transfer request would solve.

View from Peru

The coach was desperately telling everyone that they still have 180 minutes left to play, but the people of Peru celebrated long and hard after claiming a play-off spot. A typical newspaper report went something like: *Peru still dreaming of the World Cup while the Chileans will have to watch on TV. Before the game all 33 million Peruvians were nervous and paralyzed, hoping for victory. They had their hearts in their hands awaiting qualification after 36 years of hurt.* It actually said 36 years of waiting, but literalness is not the art of translation. The accompanying video clips to such reports make it clear that Peru already believed the hard work was done and would have been a very unhappy place if they had failed to trounce the All Whites.

Apparently military jets flew overhead and fireworks were set off outside the New Zealand team's hotel for the second leg in Lima. However, and despite hitting the outside of the post, the All Whites had already looked second best in Wellington and it would have been a major surprise if the team in the FIFA world rankings top 10 – Peru – had not reached Russia. There was not a major surprise. Peru dominated and only their own nerves could have got in the way. They didn't. Goal in each half. A spokesperson said, 'well yes, we cried like Italians, but for different reasons, and we'll have the best kit in Russia...yes, including the Croatian one.']

Asia

Asian qualification finishes with two groups of six teams. The top two in each qualify. And the two third -place teams play each other to earn the right to play the fourth-place team in CONCACAF. In Group A, Iran and South Korea qualified reasonably comfortably. Syria, described by a friend of mine as 'the most boring team in history', managed to secure 3rd place on goal difference. This despite only scoring nine goals and having to play all their home matches in Malaysia. To be fair to Syria, the team they edged on 13 points from 10 games, Uzbekistan scored only six goals themselves and only one team in the group (including undefeated Iran) managed more than a goal a game average: those crazy kids from South Korea banging in 11 from 10 matches. Hopes had also been high in Qatar, but they ultimately finished last and will become the first team since Japan to host a World Cup having not played previously played in one. If goals were scarce, emotion was not as Syria defied all the odds to equalise in Tehran's Azadi Stadium in front of more than 62,000 spectators in the third minute of injury time to ensure their play-off spot. If you haven't got the time to look at this, it's a man sobbing uncontrollably: https://www.youtube.com/watch?v=syy0v9ngXRU I incidentally didn't include lots of links to Latin American qualifying matches as they are generally men sobbing and screaming 'gol' and/or 'vamos al mundial'.

At some point, Australia got considered too important to lose to a South American team in World Cup qualification and was moved from Oceania to Asia. Since Israel is also playing 'outside region' perhaps Scotland could boost subsequent chances with a move elsewhere. CONCACAF would be out (Costa Rica) and South America (Peru) and Asia (Iran) but I fancy Strachan's men against Tahiti in Oceania and I reckon the Tartan Army might fancy that too. I digress. Australia lost fewer games in Group B than any other (one), but drew too many. Their Achilles heel turned out to be group whipping boys Thailand, securing only a 2-2 draw away and failing to boost their goal difference at home – in fact only securing all three points very late in the game. It allowed Saudi Arabia to sneak second place, to accompany Japan. The Saudis will be the lowest-ranked team at the tournament (FIFA's #63) apart from the hosts Russia (#65) who are ranked below Scotland, Bolivia, Haiti and the Cape Verde Islands. It meant Australia would need to beat Syria and then the fourth-placed CONCACAF team to make it to Russia. Given their records and the tension, no one was expecting a goal-fest.

Syria equalised late in the first leg of their play-off v Australia. My enthusiasm for further heroics was tempered by a twitter feed telling me all the things President Assad had done to his people and footballers, and snapped me awake at 4am to write this despite the wild celebrations the previous night which had accompanied England's qualification with that emphatic last-minute winner against Slovenia. You don't remember those wild celebrations? Just shows how wild they must have been.

What is happening in Syria is a tragedy unfolding; my twitter account tells me on a daily basis that the wrong people are killing the wrong people, and different people tell me different things. The Russians are doing bad things, say some – which I can scarcely believe. The Americans are doing worse – ditto. Assad is killing his own people. No, no: he is fighting terrorists. I am not saying it is all a matter of opinion, that there is bad on all sides etc. There is a truth and it is terrible. But, ultimately, I don't want sport to be about politics. Syria are not Assad Athletic. And while politics and death and torture are part of our sad daily reality, who you might want to win out of Syria (oppressive Assad regime) and Australia (aboriginal genocide on Tasmania, White Australia policy, treatment of migrants) is not about the things in brackets and about what is happening now or in the past. In 1966 when North Korea beat Italy it was about an underdog triumph, not first deciding whether Italy's fascist past or the unpleasantness of Kim Il-Sung should determine our support. So Syria, representing the people of Syria, equalised and still had a chance of progressing going into the return leg in Sydney.

It's not that I don't take politics seriously, but if we had to multiply scores by past crimes and government errors, England would never have a chance. Football is, after all, a game, and for most of us our allegiances are not only outside politics but hardly even a matter of choice. All the more so in the irrational, emotional world of international competition. George Orwell pointed out that England is like a family, but with the wrong people in charge. But alas still my family.

Anyway, Syria started the return leg taking the lead and finished it hitting the post. Had it gone in, Syria would have won on away goals; it was that close. As it is they lost 2-1. A brave effort indeed which did not inspire confidence in Australia ahead of their qualification eliminator against the fourth-placed CONCACAF team; a tale taken up below.

CONCACAF

The USA started the final group of six with defeat at home to Mexico and then a 4-0 spanking in San José, by Costa Rica. With 4th needed for a play-off place, qualification was not beyond them, but having performed well in recent years, they risked being a notable absentee in Russia. Going into the final round of two qualifying matches, they lay 4th, a point behind Panama and ahead of Honduras only on goal difference. Nonetheless, their fixtures looked more favourable, being at home to Panama (whom they walloped 4-0) and then away to the proverbial whipping boys of Trinidad and Tobago. In contrast, Panama's other game was at home to Costa Rica, whilst Honduras had to play the top two in the group (Costa Rica and Mexico). When Costa Rica equalised at home to Honduras in the 5th minute of injury time the USA looked, indeed were, odds-on favourites for qualification having recovered from their slow start.

And you have to say that with more footballers than any other country and more money, FIFA were probably very happy that the USA was back on track. And if the US team (two points clear with a better goal difference) were concerned about trailing 2-0 to Trinidad and Tobago at half-time, their worries will have been eased by the fact that both Panama and Honduras were losing too. A big swing was needed against the USA if they were to miss out on even a play-off spot, and when they pulled a goal back early in the second half, they also raised the possibility of getting the point they needed for automatic qualification. However, the equaliser didn't come, whilst elsewhere Honduras scored twice to beat Mexico 3-2. If Honduras were celebrating qualification and the USA worrying about a play-off, a final twist came as Panama scored an 88th-minute winner at home to Costa Rica, bumping Honduras to the play-offs and the USA out altogether. If I'd like to believe this was all 'arranged' somehow by Central American nations sometimes described as 'so far from God, so near the United States', I hope it demonstrates the opposite: that football is wonderful for its unpredictability. Panama had qualified for their first World Cup and the United States, like the Chileans, Italians and Dutch, will be watching on TV (or actually probably playing it in the park with their kids instead). Latest rumours were of them organising a tournament for 'all the good teams who didn't qualify' – presumably non-qualification upset someone's business model.

View from Panama

La Prensa: *Four years ago they were tears of pain, now they're tears of joy. There were less than five minutes left and then a goal you could hear across the entire country. The victory ended a run of 25 years without beating the Costa Ricans in WC qualifying [Ticos were attending the match in significantly smug numbers!]. This time the referee, who has been so against Panama in the past, benefited the team with a phantom equaliser which never was.*

Seriously, the 'equaliser' is a joke. Awarded by Guatemalan referee Walter López, he and his assistant must not feature in the finals for this alone. His short Wikipedia page suggests he did 2014 qualifiers but was not at the finals: https://www.youtube.com/watch?v=yifKTgb3lDo

This decision could make you think that my comment about it not being fixed is ridiculous. Also watch the winning goal if you like Latin commentators going bananas. If you don't or can't be bothered, this one said 'gol' more than 20 times before he said anything else, and that was only to say 'yes' and 'gol' intermittently for a while!]

The first leg of the play-off was in San Pedro Sula. The last time I saw a football match in Honduras it was in the capital Tegucigalpa and the pitch was of dried mud with occasional tufts of grass. But for this match the Hondurans seemed to have arranged a peat bog overlain with green cake icing. On first inspection smooth, but liable to cut up astonishingly easily. It didn't help and contributed to yet another play-off match-up in which one of the games ends 0-0. At home, however, Australia looked a different proposition. Jedinak the Aussie captain scored a hat-trick including two penalties. Figueroa the Honduran skipper responded, but deep into stoppage-time.

Oceania

Meanwhile, in the qualification campaign for men too weedy to play rugby of either code or even Aussie Rules, Samoa battled through a preliminary group only to finish bottom at the next stage with zero goals for and 19 against in three matches. In an overly elaborate scheme to see which team loses to Colombia or

Argentina (turned out to be Peru) in a play-off it looked like New Zealand or Tahiti or the Solomon Islands or Papua New Guinea might pip some even more unlikely places.

New Zealand easily qualified for the Oceania play-off from Group A but who they would play was intriguing. In a three-team group B, by the start of June 2017, Tahiti already had six points but had completed their four matches. The Solomon Islands and Papua New Guinea each had just three points each but two games remaining – home and away against each other in the local derby(ish). Two draws or a win each would send Tahiti to the play-off. If one match was a draw, whoever won the other would pip Tahiti. Excitement in PNG hadn't been as high since the signing of international relations' most wonderfully named agreement – the BIG/BRA accords[1]

In actual fact, this is what happened:

9 June (Honiara, Solomon Islands): Solomon Islands 3-2 Papua New Guinea

13 June (Port Moresby, PNG): Papua New Guinea 1-2 Solomon Islands

Tahiti's hopes were raised as PNG took the lead on 13 June, but they soon conceded a penalty and had a player sent off. And so the Oceania play-off in September was: New Zealand v Solomon Islands. The footballing world held its collective breath.

You'd think three successful penalties over two legs would be enough. But the Solomons were already 3-0 down by half-time of the away leg in Auckland, and the first of those penalties was not even enough to add respectable gloss to the 6-1 defeat. The

---

[1] If searching out what this is, you may (or may not?) wish to ensure you specify Papua New Guinea or else all manner of stuff comes up. And if you do find the right thing, be prepared for all manner of grizzly civil war stuff.

crowd of just over 10,000 is about the same as England getting 150,000 adjusted for population. Just a few days later in Honiara, not even the most optimistic islander would have been expecting a recovery, which is just as well as they conceded two quick goals to trail 1-8 on aggregate. The crowd seems unreported, although to be the equivalent of 90,000 at Wembley would have needed to be around 1000, and it's likely that was achieved. How many hung around for the tense finale after another penalty saw them make it a mere 3-8 on aggregate is unclear. It finished 2-2 on the night to claw back some respectability.

The Solomons probably needed a little divine intervention which might have come from their reserve goalkeeper, one Desmond Tutu. Ultimately though, having more players with a double 'A' in their name than Mr and Mrs Aardvark's whole family, is little consolation, though the comments section for the match includes some nice ones about their potential. Less realistic are Kiwis saying this signals the death of New Zealand rugby and predicting World Cup qualification in Buenos Aires.

In the way were not Argentinians, but Peruvians in Lima seeking to return to the glory days of Cubillas (the Peruvian Pelé and taunter-in-chief of Scots) after 36 years of hurt. The Peruvians got home comfortably.

Summary of Who Did Qualify?

(Includes Pot and World Cup Ranking at the time of Pot Distribution with a Veneer of Seriousness in Places)

Pot One

Russia (65): Despite fighting wars, doping up their sportsmen and women for decades, hazing military recruits, pickling gerbils in cherry vodka for a laugh,[1] oppressing sexual minorities, effectively banning or intimidating dissent and having inferior technical reports to other bids, Russia qualified as hosts. *(But you just said up there that we shouldn't mix politics and sport?!- Ed)*

Germany (1): Outshooting Northern Ireland only 12-8 in the

---

[1] Except that one.

game which saw them confirm qualification, the Germans were 'ruthlessly efficient and no one should write them off in the finals' (Pettiford 2004, 2006, 2016). They also had blond hair and no sense of humour and have only won the World Cup once because Westgermany was a country but which no longer exists.[2]

Brazil (2): After losing their 1st qualifying match away to Chile in October 2015, Brazil then managed just two wins from their next five qualifiers. However, they won their next eight matches in a row to be the first team apart from Russia to guarantee a place in the 2018 finals.

Portugal (3): Trailed Switzerland in qualifying after losing away. Overtook them in the last game on goal difference after beating them at home. No one else was in the frame, although The Faroe Islands came quite close to finishing above the Mighty Magyars, which is a frightening thought.

Argentina (4): Lucky. Messy. Messi.

Belgium (5): The first European team to qualify. Wins against Estonia and Gibraltar (8-1 and 9-0) suggest to me at least that European qualifying might be a hell of a lot more exciting with a narrowing down process like in Asia and Africa. Still, who could possibly object to a lovely bit of Belgium, eh?

Poland (6): Lewandowski.

France (7): On the one hand unspectacular. On the other, if you'd told me England had unspectacularly finished top of a group ahead of Sweden and Holland I'd have been jolly impressed.

---

[2] This is what happens my German friends when you decline to help me ☺

Pot Two

Spain (8): Smaller than the Scots if you'd like to explain that genetics thing again, wee Gordon? Only dropped points in a 1-1 draw in Turin and finished five points clear of Italy as a result. Impressive and they've won three out of their last five major tournaments but they're still not seeded in the top pot.

Peru (10): A team to watch and support, if only for the lovely, lovely kit.

Switzerland (11): Won nine of 10 qualifiers and still didn't qualify automatically. Still, all that luck returned against poor old Northern Ireland.

England (12): Qualified at almost the same instant as the Germans, although rather less impressively. Even so, two-thirds of the possession and 17 shots to five tell a different story from that told by the grumbling pundits. Harry Kane's late winner against Slovenia was the 2222nd of the global qualifying campaign (just in case we hadn't bored you enough already). They finished things off with the most boring game in history (away to Lithuania) which will be remembered mainly by Harry Winks.

Colombia (13): Apart from previous World Cup winners, probably the bookies' favourite to be one of Latin America's automatic qualifiers, along with Chile. But it was the Colombians who sneaked across the line this time after holding on to a point in Lima.

Mexico (16): The England of the Americas in that they are well supported by fanatical fans who frequently confuse their own enthusiasm for their team actually having a chance. Every now and again they do do quite well and people think it might be the start of something big. It isn't and they moan about the state of the game.

Uruguay (17): The country which has traditionally eschewed the 'beautiful game' in favour of ultra-violence and lunching on the opposition's neck, qualified with relative ease. After punching the ball off the line and eating Italian, let's see what the divine chipmunk can do this time.

Croatia (18): Looked like they might have the nattiest kit in the finals until Peru spoiled that one. I once said Greece had no chance of winning the 2004 Euros, so with a lump in my throat, I assure you that a team with Dejan Lovren in its defence is unlikely to win anything, ever.

Pot Three

Denmark (19): Eriksson is goooood.

Iceland (21): Presumably if a tenth of the island travelled to the Euros the place will be almost empty during the World Cup. No, wait, it's almost empty anyway because who'd want to live on a cold, potentially very hot, volcano. And they only have about 50 professional footballers to choose from. And Bjork is one of the sane ones. Well played my sson!

Costa Rica (22): By the time they were robbed in Panama, the Costa Ricans had already qualified. Ticos tend to be quite diminutive in stature (it's genetic, like Gordon Strachan) but when they get to finals they often upset someone and had a fine tournament in 2018; they emerged undefeated from a group completed by three former winners, only failing to beat the mighty England. Hmmm. They then beat former European champions Greece on penalties before losing on penalties to previous finalists Holland. Given that Holland only lost on penalties to Argentina and Argentina lost in extra time to Germany...well, Costa Rica weren't far off the pace.

Sweden (25): At least Russia will be big enough for Ibrahimovic's ego if he comes out of retirement.

Tunisia (28): Will they come back to haunt England?

Egypt (30): In final qualifying they played in front of large crowds at home with Liverpool's Salah in fine form. Salah's injury-time penalty against Congo allowed them to qualify with a game and a month to spare.

Senegal (32): Good draw, who knows?

Iran (34): In the final qualifying campaign Iran scored just eight goals in their first eight games. But having conceded none that was enough for six wins, two draws and qualification with still two games remaining. They drew their final two games.

Pot Four

Serbia (38): Other teams will be as frightened of Serbia as players are of Dušan Tadić in the Premier League. Only a very little bit.

Nigeria (41): One might have expected Cameroon or Algeria to put up more of a showing, but they didn't and the Super Eagles – who've never really soared at finals – made it to Russia with a game to spare.

Australia (43): It is my nightmare that like Hungary or Scotland, England will one day be the laughing stock of international football, and Australia will dominate, contesting World Cup finals with Germany on a regular basis. Still, they will be my 29th favourite team at the finals.

Japan (44): The mighty Maya Yoshida has scored 10 times for Japan in around 80 appearances. He scored in qualifying in the 4-0 home win v Thailand. At the time of writing he looks like the only player capable of scoring for Southampton.

Morocco (48): Who will be their secret squirrel?

Panama (49): Maybe even more unlikely than Iceland's qualification, especially given their 4-0 loss to the USA in their crucial-looking penultimate qualifier. Relied on team spirit, national unity, luck and a Guatemalan referee who could actually see things happening before his eyes that couldn't have happened. ¡Bien jugado, muchachos!

South Korea (62): Qualifying for the finals was a nice distraction from being the filling in a loony sandwich with Kim Jong-Un leader of the DPRK and Donald Trump playing chicken over who's going to destroy Seoul/start World War Three.[3]

Saudi Arabia (63): This will be the Saudis' fifth finals, having qualified consecutively in 1994, 1998, 2002 and 2006. Apart from qualification at the expense of the Aussies, 2017 was a great year.

---

[3] Placeholder for the latest amazing thing Trump does without being kicked out for the ridiculous narcissistic racist (etc.) he is. Have you seen the clip of him aggressively asserting how humble he is?

A man decided women might be allowed to drive. Whatever next? Men loving men and women loving women, dancing in a skirt, not believing in God, being allowed to keep your head for these things, not encouraging extremism!? One of Britain's most important allies.

Qualifiers by Group –

(without any Veneer of Seriousness)

Group A

Country: Russia

Tournament history

The glory days were all back in the Soviet Union era, so if I try to claim that Russia won the European Championship back in 1960 and finished fourth in the 1966 World Cup (or even if they might have won in 1958 but for locking up their best player), my co-author will go apoplectic, given his intransigent insistence that Germany has only won one World Cup. Russia did reach the semi-finals of Euro 2008, though, losing to eventual winners Spain.

How does the national league shape up?

It features a good sprinkling of the clubs you've heard of from Champions' League and Europa League involvement, mainly located in the city of Moscow. Spartak Moscow are the most recent winners of the Russian Premier League, preceded by monotonous success by CSKA Moscow and Zenit St Petersburg, with a couple of cameos by Rubin Kazan. It's a pretty solid league (unable to contain or control racism, to be frank) but doesn't set the world alight. Same as the national team, really.

Manager / Coach

We've been cruelly denied the presence, and dodgy punning potential, of Leonid Slutsky, who scampered off to Hull City after Euro 2016 (and only lasted six months there). We're left with Stanislav Cherchesov, who is obligingly reminiscent of pretty much any mid-20th Century European dictator you'd care to name (and a couple of Spanish national coaches since). He has proved to be a reassuring influence on the unfortunately named fitness coach, Vladimir Panikov. Fans of non-anagrams will be interested to learn that 'Stanislav Cherchesov' comes out as 'Snowball in hell's chance, mate'.

Players to watch

At the time of writing, the Russian squad is made up entirely of players based in Russia, with only three exceptions: one each in Belgium, Germany and Turkey, where their movements can be closely monitored. We don't, therefore, get much of an opportunity to watch Russian players week-on-week in other European leagues. In the tournament this summer, we confidently predict that any goals are likely to come from the colourful boots of Fyodor Smolov and Aleksandr Kokorin (neither of whom notched a single goal in Euro 2016, despite an identical prediction back then).

Any ringers?

The squad for the World Cup is likely to include Brazilian-born goalkeeper Guillerme and full-back Mário Fernandes. We couldn't possibly comment on rumours that both players were robustly 'persuaded' to take out Russian citizenship by the NKVD/KGB/FSB.

The word on the street

There's plenty of cockiness visible in the press and on the chat forums, with Russian fans reckoning they've got a pretty good chance on home soil. Some more reflective accounts suggest concern about the likelihood of hooliganism, and that's obviously a view shared by fans of many nations.

Player lookalikes (aka 'any dead-ringers')

Igor Akinfeev still looks like Steve Harper, you'll be pleased to hear. Aleksandr Samedov recently auditioned unsuccessfully for the remake of *Rentaghost*, and just before Christmas Magomed Ozdoyev was outed as Amir Khan's distant cousin in the Russian version of *I'm an industrious midfielder, get me out of here*. Perhaps most controversially, Alan Dzagoev could easily be the son of Roman Abramovich.

Player anagrams

Viktor Vasin = Vino VAT Risk

Igor Smolnivok = So Liking Vroom

Songs to sing in the Fan Zone

It's tempting to wind up the hosts by belting out an uneasy medley of the Beatles' 'Back in the USSR', Boney M's 'Rasputin' and Billy Joel's 'Leningrad'. Anyone eager to show off their swing/punk crossover credentials can chip in with Matt Monroe's 'From Russia with Love' and the Vibrators' 'Moscow Disco'. Anything by the Arctic Minskis? No?

Our prediction

They'll probably get through the group then crumble in the last 16.

....

Country: Saudi Arabia

Tournament history

The Falcons reached the Round of 16 in the 1994 World Cup. Otherwise, they've had some regional success as past winners of the AFC Asian Cup, Arab Nations Cup, Gulf Cup of Nations and Islamic Solidarity Games. So no slouches, but despite a good, disciplined and much improved style of play in recent years, they're unlikely to shine in this tournament. You heard it here first. The worst ranked team in the tournament apart from Russia – sorry, did we already say that?

Tell us a bit about the national league

It's just over 40 years old now, and has developed a pyramid structure. Al-Hilal are the reigning champions. Of the 14 teams currently in the top flight, only Ohod, based in Medina, do not bear the prefix 'Al'. Perhaps cashing in on this linguistic quirk, there are unsubstantiated rumours that Al Jolson, Al Capone, Al Gore and Al Murray Pub Landlord have launched audacious franchise bids for next season. (Oh, that's just silly! -Ed).

Manager / Coach

Argentinian Juan Antonio Pizzi is the current incumbent, replacing his compatriot Edgardo Bauza, who lasted two months in 2017. The back catalogue of national coaches includes such luminaries as Ferenc Puskás and Bill McGarry, so quality has clearly been sought at all times. Pizzi is notable for his name not being the plural of 'pizza', and for his refusal to yield to multiple pleas of 'get a bloody haircut, hippy'.

Players to watch

Most of the likely squad will be unfamiliar to UK football fans, with only a small handful of recent call-ups playing abroad (mainly in Spain). For comedy value, keep an eye on 41-year-old Hussein Abdulghani, and for goal-scoring prowess, it would be wise not to underrate Taisir Al-Jassim, Mohammad Al-Shalhoub, Nasser Al-Shamrani and Mohammad Al-Sahlawi who, as mentioned early-doors, knocked five past East Timor in qualifying.

The word on the street

It was tricky to nail down any precise predictions from local footy fans, but the bloke two doors down from me has just got back from neighbouring Dubai, where he claimed to have engaged a Saudi family in conversation, and the son had apparently been representative of a surging wave of optimism back home. I also once knew a Saudi student on a government scholarship who didn't have a bad word to say about his country or its national team.

Player anagrams

Ahmed Assiri = Messi Hair Ad

Ali Al-Nemer = A Lean Miler

Ibrahim Ghaleb = Me Big Hair Ball

Hassan Kadesh = Has Shaken Sad

Nooh Al-Mousa = Homo au Salon

Songs to sing in the Fan Zone

We could skip jauntily through the back catalogues of Riyadh-na (though an umbrella is unlikely to be needed in Saudi Arabia) or chirpily annoying Irish twins Jeddah-ward, though we're not sure how well this would go down locally. Perhaps ABC's 'Tabuk of Love' or Jason Derulo's 'Qatif'. Bloody hell! That last one was almost contemporary. (Could we have one that almost makes sense? –Ed.)

Our prediction

Group A is finely balanced, and on paper any of the four teams could go through. I'm going for Saudi Arabia to keep it tight and scrape through to meet their doom in the Round of 16, but only if they can take a point off Uruguay. This could get tricky. (Your co-author thinks they'll go out at this stage, which is a convenient hedge-betting tool!)

Country: Egypt

Tournament history

The Pharaohs (who obviously emerged from the Egyptian league's pyramid system – oh, come on, that was an open goal) have qualified for, or played in, the World Cup finals on only two previous occasions: 1934 and 1990. They won the Africa Cup of Nations as recently as 2010, and have an impressive record in that competition.

Manager / Coach

Argentinian Héctor Cúper is a well-known figure from his years managing in Spain. He really should have, but wasn't, nicknamed 'Mini' or 'Tommy' at school in Santa Fe. His earlier work as a police surgeon earned him the soubriquet 'The Cop Curer', which is coincidentally an anagram of his name. (If in doubt about the truth of any of this, go and see a doctor, -Ed).

Where do Egypt stand in the league of 'number of letters dropping below the baseline of a font'?

They're currently ranked top of the pile, with an impressive 60% of the letters in their country's name descending below the line on which they're written. That could be a meaningful omen in World Cup terms. Or maybe not. (Actually, your co-author thinks you should go and see a doctor!)

Players to watch

Inevitably and rightly, most of the attention will be focused on Liverpool's Mohamed Salah, who has been a revelation since signing for the Anfield outfit. Will he rise to the occasion, or will the pressure be too much for him to handle? Is there any point in padding this text with rhetorical questions? Salah aside, there are another half dozen players currently based in England, including two (Hegazi and Gabr) at West Brom. However, both statistically and in terms of current form, all eyes will be on Salah to spearhead the goal-scoring quest. At the time of writing he has 32 goals from 56 internationals, and nobody else in recent squads has scored more than six.

The word on the street

I was recently introduced to an Egyptian PhD student on a university campus. He was buoyant about his country's chances in Russia but only, he stressed, if Salah can avoid injury – 'otherwise we're buggered'. I applauded his knowledge of colloquial English and bought him a nice cup of tea.

Player lookalikes

The appropriateness of Salah moving to Liverpool was highlighted by fans with longer memories pointing out his resemblance to Lucien (actor Michael Angelis) from *The Liver Birds*. Hardworking former Hull City favourite Ahmed Elmohamady is defined as 'any earnest young copper keen to make his mark in *The Bill*'.

Player anagrams

Ahmed Fathy = Hey Daft Ham

Ramy Rabia = A Barmy Air

Tarek Hamed = Head Market

Songs to sing in the Fan Zone

All sorts of bouncy stuff here, from The Bangles' 'Walk Like an Egyptian' to the Madness stomper 'Night Boat to Cairo'. You've also got back catalogues by Alexandria Burke, Biffy Cairo, Cleopatra and Nile Rodgers, plus some hitherto unacknowledged solo work by legendary Black Sabbath bassist Giza Butler. But if what you're actually asking is whether I can produce any *really* shit puns, the answer would have to be: 'Ride a White Aswan' by T Rex or Paul Young's 'Love of the Tutankhamun People'. (Genius! -Ed)

Our prediction

A side worthy of progression to the knockout stages, but we fear there may be too much reliance on Salah, so it's a group-stage exit.

....

Country: Uruguay

Tournament history

We know from our history, and from Lloyd Pettford's indefatigable research, that Uruguay rode the waves of sulkiness to take the early World Cup competitions by storm (when they chose to enter, that is). In more recent times, the boys in sky blue can point to having reached the semi-finals in South Africa in 2010. Given the size of the country, Uruguay has punched above its weight (and over the bar v Ghana in 2010's quarter-final) more consistently than surely any other team.

Manager / Coach

Óscar Tabárez has had a host of managerial posts across the Spanish-speaking world, as well as a couple in Italy, so he's not lacking in experience. This is his second spell at the helm of the national team, and his first in charge of the potentially fiery Luis Suárez. With a background in teaching, Tabárez is reputed to take no prisoners in instilling squad discipline, so the punching and the biting and the cheating may be coming to an end. Although knowing Uruguay, compulsory.

We know about Luis Suárez, but is the national league any good?

Peñarol and Nacional are the two biggies in a 16-strong top division, a staggering 13 of whom are based in the capital Montevideo. Both Peñarol and Nacional are multiple winners of the Copa Libertadores, but have not tasted success in that competition since the late 1980s.

Players to watch

The Smash & Grab (or Smashie and Not-Nicey?) pairing of Cavani and Suárez up-front has served Uruguay very well in recent years, but now (we confidently predict) is the time for Hull City's Abel Hernández to step out of their shadows and have the tournament of his life, before being poached by Manchester City and being left on the bench for the next three years. In the non-existent glossary, you'll find 'confidently predict' translates as 'we haven't got a clue but even if people read this before the tournament, who is likely to return afterwards?'

The word on the street

No shortage of opinions reached us via older Spanish and Italian friends whose wider family moved to Uruguay at various points in the 20th Century. Most coincided in asserting (with varying degrees of aggressively emphatic body language) that the glory days of 1930/50 are going to be revived in Russia. Suárez is on fire, they claim, and will be unstoppable. I'll leave that one to sink in (like your man's fangs). When a Uruguayan defender hacks the Achilles of a 19-year-old play-maker or rugby tackles outside the box to protect a lead, remember that after nibbling on an Italian defender and being sent home in 2014, Suárez returned not as a Beckham/1998-esque villain but as a complete hero.

Player lookalikes

Cristian Rodríguez is the unacknowledged third member of 80s pop duo Tears for Fears, while Diego Godín is a no-nonsense head of maths in an inner-city Birmingham comprehensive school. Álvaro González is gainfully employed as a stunt double for Rafa Nadal when the occasion demands, which admittedly isn't often. The niggling paternity case involving Steven Gerrard and Uruguayan midfielder Federico Valverde looks unlikely to be resolved before the tournament starts.

Player anagrams

Edinson Cavani = Dances in a Vino

Martín Silva = Vain as Trim

Esteban Conde = See Conte Band

Songs to sing in the Fan Zone

Much of the soundtrack from *The Full Montevideo* could probably be played over the speakers here, with cameos by Salto-N-Pepa. The timeless 'Uruguay So Vain' by Carly Simon could also be rolled out, as could Queen's 'Another One Bites the Full-back'.

Our prediction

Should get through OK, but must be wary against Egypt and Saudi Arabia in the group. Progress thereafter will very much depend on who they line up against in the Round of 16, as they've been known to freeze on the big occasions.

....

Group B

Country: Portugal

Tournament history

Portugal's stock is high at present following their Euro 2016 triumph. However, recent World Cups have produced lacklustre performances, to say nothing of a couple of shocking embarrassments. As in all tournaments over the last decade, much will depend on Cristiano Ronaldo's form, fitness and level of indifference. Their 2016 win was at least partly attributable to the ever reliable centre-half José Fonte; well, he was ever reliable until he left Southampton and joined West Ham, at which point he turned into an East End cart-horse on whom it would be unwise to rely (unless you're Chinese).

Manager / Coach

Fernando Santos hasn't mellowed the notably threatening glower he sported two years ago in Euro 2016, but if it helped him to guide his side to a memorable victory in the final against hosts France, then it's obviously worth keeping. A subsequent third place in the 2017 Confederations Cup did his reputation no harm, either.

Can the Portuguese league ever regain its majestic status?

There's a chance. Why it's currently ranked a lowly seventh among European leagues is something of a mystery, given the relative buoyancy of the national team and the number of star players with whom we're familiar. But that's the thing: so many of them are playing abroad. Fewer than a third of players called up for recent squads are playing in Portugal.

Players to watch

Manuel Fernandes and Eder currently play in Russia, so should receive either a warm or a freezing welcome from the fans of the host nation. It'll be interesting to see how the England-based trio of Bernardo Silva, João Mário and Rubén Neves fare on the big stage. However, we're predicting a democratic sharing-out of the goals between veteran Bruno Alves and new kid on the block André Silva. (Somehow my co-author's extensive research missed out Swansea's Renato Sanches – you just can't get the staff! At the age of 18 he became the youngest player to play for Portugal in an international tournament, and the youngest to win a Euro Final, in 2016).

Have Portuguese haircut trends kept up with international norms?

Very much so. André Silva and Gelson Martins constitute the vanguard in this department. (Presumably 'Random' Fitzsimons knows what this means!)

The word on the street

We got bored with contacts bleating on about Ronaldo, so spent a few minutes feeding a couple of emails through Google Translate into Portuguese and back into English. This produced the revelatory news that the Portuguese selection 'has all the possibilities of the world to vanquish all the cream that is placed before it, and to play with intensity but also with much tranquility in all the large parts of the field.'

Player lookalikes

Goalkeeper Beto has always struck me as having the kind of face you see appearing in a 'swaggering geezer' guise in the Channel 4 smash *First Dates*. When João Mário smiles, he bears a passing reference to a much younger newsreader Darren Jordon, which is no bad thing.

Player anagrams

Rony Lopes = Pylon Rose

André Gomes = Same Donger

Nélson Oliveira = Love Loin in Arse

Songs to sing in the Fan Zone

You could start off with 'Feel it Still' by Portugal The Man, and move on to Jack Savoretti's 'Bragabond', via some lilting work by Cole Porto and possibly 'So Faro Away' by Dire Straits / Dire Puns.

Our prediction

No problem in getting through the group, alongside Spain. Destined to come a cropper in the quarter-finals.

....

Country: Spain

Tournament history

Serious domination in the biggies between 2008 and 2012 (plus second place in the 2013 Confederations Cup), but a bit of a tail-off thereafter. The squad is in place, the underlying quality indisputable, so it would be ill-advised to write them off. They are the new Germans in this respect, but with more breaks, more things done tomorrow and slightly healthier snacks.

Is the Spanish domestic league in good shape?

Ain't that the truth. Or at least it is at the top end. Barcelona and the two Madrids are still forces to be reckoned with on the European stage, but notwithstanding plucky efforts by the likes of Valencia and Sevilla there's a bit of a gulf further down the table.

Manager / Coach

Youthful-looking Basque Julen Lopetegui cut a swathe through the interminable list of moustachioed bigots and fat bastards who had preceded him (in the queue at the local bakery, I mean: for legal reasons we can't cast any nasturtiums on the characters of the recent coaches of the national team). For anyone unfamiliar with Lopetegui, think 'a quietly confident but slightly less opinionated Gary Neville'.

Players to watch

We know all the main players from Champions League exposure, so let's limit this to a set of bold predictions: Morata and Silva will flop in Russia; Gerard Deulofeu will play out of his skin, and Isco will come from nowhere and either win, or come close to winning, the Golden Boot. 'Bold Predictions' appears in our mythical glossary as 'so much nonsense'.

The word on the street

A table-full of Spaniards at a branch of Costa in Leeds concurred that, whilst the glory days appear to be behind them, the Spanish team can still cut it internationally – see their impressive road to qualification, when they notched nine wins and a draw out of ten games, comfortably relegating Italy to second place. The mood is buoyant. *Mucho cockio*, as they don't say.

Player lookalikes

Álvaro Odriozola is Eddie Tenpole Tudor's great-nephew. Alberto Moreno has successfully completed his visual scallification procedure at Liverpool, but some critics have argued that his hairstyle still needs work. In a previous book, I argued that David Silva was Duncan from Blue, but then he went and shaved his head. What is a lookalike-spotter to do? Simply return to dodgy kidnapping-and-subsequent-paternity plots by observing that Asier Illarramendi's mother was intercepted by Icelandic pirates in 1989, blah blah blah. (Good job there isn't a paper shortage or you'd be arrested for that! -Ed)

Player anagrams

Diego Costa = I Co-eat Dogs

Pedro = Doper/E-Prod/Poder

Andrés Iniesta = Serie A in Stand

Songs to sing in the Fan Zone

Start your quest with anything by The Kings of León. There are plenty of songs performed by Noel and Liam Málaga to provide an Oasis of calm on a hot Russian day. Or you could have 'Córdoba the Wind' by The Stereophonics, 'Barça the Dutchie' by Musical Youth or Green Day's 'Good Madriddance (Time of Your Life)'.

Our prediction

Semis at least. I think we'll see them back to top form in the international arena.

....

Country: Morocco

Tournament history

A smattering of successful World Cup qualifications, but no progress from the group stage since 1986. On that basis, we shouldn't expect a lot, but they did win the 2018 African Nations Championship, walloping Nigeria 4-0 in the final, so current form looks impressive. Possibly swindled out of a previous African World Cup by a possibly corrupt FIFA and so possibly hosting one in the not so distant future. But you didn't hear that from us, as with so much of interest to sinister Eastern Europeans with umbrellas, and lawyers.

Manager / Coach

'Rev. Hardener' (or Frenchman 'Hervé Renard' to give him his real-life, non-anagramised form) is a widely experienced coach, having managed national sides across Africa, plus clubs in France and China (and, as a predictably essential step in any such trajectory: Cambridge United). His tactical acumen is undisputed, having masterminded triumphant Africa Cup of Nations campaigns with Zambia (2012) and the Ivory Coast (2015). If you're unsure what he looks like, flick through your mental images of 'any cocky Australian tennis coach from the 1980s'.

Players to watch

Ayoub El Kaabi up-front has hit the ground running, having notched up (at the time of writing) nine goals in his first six international appearances. Goals could also come from Youssef El-Arabi and perhaps vice-captain Mbark Boussoufa, who operates in midfield. Not too much likelihood of English-based involvement: just Romain Saïss (Wolves) and Sofiane Boufal (Southampton).

So are all the squad members pukka Moroccans, or are any of them dodgy ringers?

Don't be absurd – they're all proper Moroccans. Oh, except Romain Saïss. And Manuel da Costa, now that you come to mention it. You never got any of this type of caper in the days of Tony Cascarino, to be sure, to be sure.

Can we be sure there will be due diligence paid to on-trend facial hair?

For sure. Fouad Chafik is the squad representative in this sense, charged with ensuring that beard-trimming meets with internationally accepted norms.

The word on the street

Whilst there's a general acceptance that it's going to be hard to get past the twin giants of Spain and Portugal in the group, there's a strategic thread that suggests that if those two draw with each other, there might be a way for Morocco to play out of their skins in their three games and squeeze through. I should point out that this 'strategic thread' was conveyed to me way past midnight at a party in Hull, by a stoned Moroccan bloke with the glassiest eyes I've ever seen. He did confirm, however, that his utterances were bona fide 'mots de la rue'.

Player lookalikes

Ronnie O'Sullivan's frequent indifference at (and occasional absence from) major snooker tournaments is explained by his moonlighting as Moroccan goalkeeper Yassine Bounou. Salaheddine Saidi is wisely preparing for life after football by enrolling at the Russell Brand Lookalike Academy. Reports suggest he's doing well, but hasn't managed to pull Katy Perry yet.

Player anagrams

Anas Zniti = Nazi Saint

Amine Harit = Haitian R.E.M.

Nabil Dirar = Blair Drain

Youssef El-Arabi = Uf! Sore Labia? Yes!

Songs to sing in the Fan Zone

Status Quo's 'Moroccan All Over the World' should get the party started, with the tempo maintained by Chas and Dave's 'Rabat', Plastic Bertrand's 'Safi Plane Pour Moi' and Black Lace's 'Agadir'. Any requests to the DJ for more up-to-date material will be instantly rewarded with a quick spin of Lady Gaga's 'Poker Fez'.

Our prediction

On balance, Portugal and Spain are going to be too strong. Group stage exit.

....

Country: Iran

Tournament history

This will be Iran's fifth foray into World Cup finals territory, hard on the heels of their 2014 qualification, but they have never progressed past the group stage. That said, their presence in the 32-team tournament in Russia is fully merited, given their position of 32nd in the most recent FIFA rankings. Alas they will be unable to repeat their 1998 defeat of the 'Great Satan' (USA) as Satan didn't qualify.

How do they fare in regional terms?

Their CV boasts considerable success at regional, continental and intercontinental levels, but nothing to shout about in the last ten years. Much is made of their rivalries with Iraq, Saudi Arabia and South Korea, which clearly have sprung from very different geographical and political, as well as sporting origins.

Manager / Coach

Fans of Manchester United – of whom there are a few dotted around the world, allegedly with concentration spikes in the Home Counties – will be familiar with the benign bulldog Carlos Queiroz. He has enjoyed notable renown and success as a coach, and his teams are always well organised and full of flair. The same can be said for his hair.

Players to watch

Most of the squad is home-based, with a sprinkling plying their trade around European leagues, including three in Russia. At the time of writing, only one squad player is based in the English league: captain Ashkan Dejagah, who plays for Nottingham Forest. (Aw, can't we put Notts Forest? I know they like it...)

The word on the street

Trust me when I tell you that I did try very hard to make contact with Iranian fans. In the end, it boiled down to a thrice-removed contact, whose view on the team's chances in Russia was along the lines of 'we've got no chance, and the whole country knows it'.

Player lookalikes

Goalkeeper Alireza Beiranvand could offer facial similarity to most of his post-war Italian counterparts, while midfield general Saeid Ezatolahi earns handy money deputising for celebrity Iain Lee when the latter is on jungle duty. Captain Ashkan Dejagah has recently acknowledged that his days standing on either end of the Boyzone line-up, looking moody in an overcoat, are sadly behind him.

Player non-anagrams

Amir Abedzadeh = 'Unlikely to get a game in goal'

Sardar Azmoun = 'OK, top goalscorer but mostly against crap teams'

Hamed Lak = 'Ham Dalek or Made Dhal, sorry they're actually anagrams'

Songs to sing in the Fan Zone

What better way to start than with The Crystals' seminal 'Da Doo Iran Iran', backed up by Madonna's 'Like a Persian'? Tehranosaurus Rex might have some useful input as background music here.

Our prediction

Group-stage exit.

....

Group C

Country: France

Tournament history

It's 20 years now since les Bleus triumphed on home soil in the 1998 World Cup, and 12 since they lost to Italy in the final in Germany in 2006. More recently and meaningfully, they lost to Portugal in the final of Euro 2016, so their current form isn't too shabby.

Manager / Coach

Didier Deschamps has hung on grimly, resisting all urges to resign and withstanding being labelled 'a stunt double for Bobby Davro' in a previous book of this type. He is now being rebranded as an ageing rock star on permanent stand-by duty in case either of the minor members of A-Ha ever falls ill.

Are the French players in the English league representative of the quality and temperament of the French national team?

Pretty much, yes.

Players to watch

Like it or not, it's going to be all about the central spine of Lloris, Varane, Pogba and whichever of Giroud or Griezmann can be arsed to get out of bed. However, let's all keep an eye on Antony Martial, for whom the time is right to make a wider impact.

The word on the street

A few words, for sure, but also plenty of shoulder-shrugging. Confidence is understandably high, particularly after Euro 2016, and in fact we didn't come across a single view that suggested the French weren't going to make the final. Don't expect too much overt, *pas-cool* enthusiasm until it looks like they might win, though.

Player lookalikes

Check out Christophe Jallet when he joins the cast of *EastEnders* this autumn as a hitherto unknown, 'tasty' cousin of Phil Mitchell who thrives on being invited to 'sort it out'. Kevin Gameiro is any *Blue Peter* presenter post-1990 (except Konnie Huq).

Do the French players still hold the annual 'Je suis plus sulky que vous' competition that started back in the 1970s?

Yes. It's a bit lower-profile than it used to be, but it's still sorted out over the course of a tetchy lunch in Marseille each spring. Dimitri Payet is the current holder.

Songs to sing in the Fan Zone

Gloria Estefan's 'I Don't Want Toulouse You Now' would kick us off with a powerful ballad to shrug our shoulders to, followed by Roy Orbison's 'In Reims' and Daft Punk's 'Toulon'. Perhaps the tournament-stealing anthem, though, would be 'Cannes You Dig It?' by The Mock Turtles. (Co-author attempts to join in with 'Long Road to Rouen' by The Foo Fighters and 'Have a Nice Day' by The Stereophonics.)

Our prediction

Semis.

....

Country: Australia

Tournament history

2018 will be the fourth consecutive finals appearance for Australia, after their much publicised debut in 1974. However, despite recent buoyancy of form, they've only got out of the group once, in 2006. Success in minor competitions doesn't convince us that they've really gelled as a squad, despite the relative abundance of individual 'characters'.

Manager / Coach

Coach Bert van Marwijk has been heavily criticised for failing to choose between two clear options: declaring his hand (or face) as either Ian Rush or Ian 'Pike' Lavender. (Stupid boy! -Ed) This may cost him dear if the Socceroos don't advance from the group stage.

Players to watch

We can be sure of one thing: Tim Cahill will give it absolutely everything in his World Cup swansong, both on the pitch and off. His goal-scoring record for his country is phenomenal, but what is lacking is consistent back-up in this department: maybe captain Mile Jedinak will add a few from midfield.

Is there any rhyme or reason to the 'where are all the players based?' conundrum? Can we see patterns developing?

No, it's still 'mental' (technical term). Recent squads have included players based in Japan, South Korea, Turkey, Saudi Arabia, China, Israel and Hull. We love it.

The word on the street

'G'Day'.

Any proper answer?

OK. Three correspondents got in touch, two of whom focused entirely on Tim Cahill and his likelihood of blasting his way to the Golden Boot. The third guy was considerably more measured, responding that France would win the group easily, with serious nip-and-tuck between Australia, Peru and Denmark for second place. This is very much how we see it, too.

Player lookalikes

Bradford City defender Ryan McGowan's transition into a low-budget Kevin Kilbane is scheduled to be complete by Christmas 2018, so we may see a 'work in progress' version on the field in Russia. Don't let this alarm you. Mark Milligan, meanwhile, vehemently denies that he is a reconstituted Tony Adams. Fans of 90s music are catered for with the inclusion of Aziz Behich, aka Danny Goffey, the drummer from Supergrass.

But do any of the squad look like Nottingham supermarkets, you say?

Only Trent Sainsbury.

Player anagrams

Milos Degenek = Like Dog Semen

Ryan Edwards = Sane Dry Ward

Ajdin Hrustic = Can I DJ? Ur Shit

Songs to sing in the Fan Zone

None of the clichéd Oz classic anthems will be allowed, unless you happen to be from Australia. We therefore need to look to new-fangled ditties like Bart Simpson's 'Do the Hobart Man', Altered Images' 'Happy Perthday' or Duffy's 'Adelaide Devotion', or the wealth of undiscovered work by Aztec Canberra.

Our prediction

Sorry, but despite herculean efforts by Tim Cahill and his merry men, second place in the group behind France will go to Denmark.

....

Country: Peru

Tournament history

The White and Red Incans reached the last eight of the World Cup a couple of times in the 1970s, but have not qualified for the finals since 1982. There have been a couple of recent semi-final appearances in the Copa América, hinting at a decent level of form. So will 2018 be their year? No. (Or yes, possibly.)

Does the country meet the 50% threshold for vowels in its name?

Yes, by a whisker.

Manager / Coach

Another Argentinian coach: this time Ricardo Gareca. He's done a good job at club level in various parts of Latin America, but the Peru gig is his first foray into international management. I know you're crying out here for one of my 'very specific' lookalikes, so here you go: Bill Nighy playing Bjorn Borg in an ill-advised comedy biopic.

Players to watch

Only one UK-based Peruvian has featured in recent squads, I'm afraid: André Carrillo at Watford. Otherwise, most of the squad is based in the major Latin American leagues, with a sprinkling in continental Europe. The twin scoring threats are likely to be Jefferson Farfán and Paolo Guerrero.

Can you translate some of the players' names into English with 'hilarious' results, please?

Go on then:

Pedro Gallese = Peter Welsh (oh aye, feckin' hilarious, Ronan!)

Andy Polo = Andy Ice Lolly

Pedro Aquino = Peter Not Here

Iván Bulos = Ivan Unfounded Rumours

Paolo Guerrero = Paul Warrior

Jefferson Farfán – Ex US President wafts himself from a distance (more absurd than hilarious?)

That's more than enough, thanks.

OK.

The word on the street (apart from '¡Sí, se puede!')

Overwhelming confirmations of the national team's plan to go out there and enjoy the experience, with no expectations of any level of success. Sporting philosophy at its finest. (Except, like England, when push comes to shove they'll take it far too seriously.)

Player lookalikes

Alberto Junior Rodríguez is Danny from Hear'Say, whereas Aldo Corzo bears a passing resemblance to the late, great and much missed Gary Speed. Yoshimar Yotún ('Y-Fronts', to his teammates) is advancing well in his quest to look like Alexis Sánchez, although his request for identical wages was apparently turned down this season.

Player anagrams

Andy Polo = Loopy Dan

Diego Penny = Yon Deep Gin

Pedro Aquino = Dear Quin Poo

Leao Butrón = On a Trouble

Songs to sing in the Fan Zone

The one that'll be on everybody's lips (possibly even Simon

Cowell's) is Sinitta's 'So Machu Picchu'. Beyond that, there are classics like The Monkees' 'Daydream Be-Lima' and The Spice Girls' 'Peru Do You Think You Are?' and artists whose back catalogues we could plunder, such as Andes Williams. (Honestly, you're a proper Titicaca at times. -Ed).

Our prediction

Lots of patronising descriptions of Peru's brave effort, and maybe at least one draw in the group stage, but we can't see them progressing. Lovely kit, though.

....

Country: Denmark

Tournament history

Their World Cup highpoint was reaching the quarter-finals in 1998, but they failed to qualify in 2014. Elsewhere, they have the barmy record of having won the 1992 European Championship without having qualified for it, and clinching the 1995 Confederations Cup on the only occasion they've ever been in it. Expect the unexpected.

Manager / Coach

Norwegian (and former Manchester City player) Åge Hareide is at the helm in Denmark these days, where he enjoys life as a baffling hybrid of Chris Tarrant, former Labour MP Alan Johnson and any dodgy business associate of Arthur Daley in *Minder*.

Players to watch

Peter Schmeichel, Michael Laudrup, Allan Simonsen and Jon Dahl Tomasson. Sorry, cut-and-paste malfunction. OK: solid defence from Simon Kjær, free-scoring midfield contributions from Christian Eriksen and punchy prowess up-front from Nicklas Bendtner, who needs no introductions in the UK.

I'm sure they all speak excellent English, but please could you throw in one or two non-Danish-sounding squad names, to keep us on our toes? If you could make it sound like they're from Yorkshire or Ireland, that would be even better.

My pleasure: Martin Braithwaite and Thomas Delaney.

They're Scandies, so they must have the on-trend hairstyle thing nailed, yeah?

How astute. Yes, much evidence of excessive 'product' deployment, so have no worries there.

The word on the street

Wonderful (x2) Copenhagen was apparently empty when I met up with a tableful of noisy Danes in Milton Keynes recently. We talked at length about 'hygge', and it gradually dawned on me that these guys weren't footy fans. One of them was aware Denmark had qualified, and he said he thought they had a good chance. He was both pissed and deluded.

Player lookalikes

Simon Kjær is the member of A-Ha you never hear much about these days, while elsewhere in BoyBandiLandia, Jens Stryger

Larsen is at least 25% of A1, and probably nearer 75%.

Player anagrams

Jonas Lössi = Jon Soil Ass

Lasse Vibe = Base Elvis

Pione Sisto = Is Too Penis

Songs to sing in the Fan Zone

Dane Vera Lynn and Debbie Harry of Brøndby deserve a moment of musical respect here before we turn our attention to 'Aarhus' by Madness and 'Ballerup to the Bumper' by Grace Jones.

Our prediction

Will scrape through the group with France, but will be seriously found out in the Round of 16.

....

Group D

Country: Argentina

Tournament history

Argentina's World Cup record of two wins (most recently in 1986) and three lost finals (spanning the years 1930 to 2014) seems somehow unsatisfactory, given the country's footballing reputation and array of gifted individual players. (Err, no, it seems unsatisfactory given the amount of cheating they've done, surely? Handball, fouling, diving, drug-taking, bribery, torture – no seriously, see 1978. -Ed). They have a sprinkling of success in continental competitions, but less so in recent years; tellingly, they've failed to qualify for seven of the last eight Confederations Cups and almost didn't make this World Cup. We should never write them off, though.

Manager / Coach

Jorge Sampaoli has both club and international experience to bring to his current role in charge of his home country's *selección nacional*. His sides are always well organised, with good team spirit.

Players to watch

It's difficult to begin anywhere other than with Agüero and Messi, who've both been on sparkling form this season. Ángel di Maria and Gonzalo Higuaín can still do a job, if they're given the space to do so. Otamendi and Mascherano are likely to remain reliably waterproof at the back.

Can we be sure of the correct dosages of fiery temperaments and other sundry Latin clichés?

Indeed.

The word on the street

Unsurprisingly, there are great hopes that *La Albiceleste* can go one better than in 2014 and win the trophy in 2018. Unsurprisingly, talk centres around Messi. I think the real debate would start if Messi and Agüero were both injured.

Player lookalikes

Goalkeeper Nahuel Guzmán is Peter Shilton without the dodgy perm. Former Liverpool favourite Emiliano Insúa is any member of Oasis whose surname wasn't Gallagher. Enzo Pérez and Sergio Agüero are brothers.

Player anagrams

Lucas Alario = O Casual Liar

Diego Perotti = I Go To Pee Dirt

Leandro Paredes = A Slade Ponderer

Songs to sing in the Fan Zone

'Sugar Sugar' by The Argies or 'La Pampa' by Ritchie Valens? OK, let's get a bit more highbrow: you may recall 'Mulder and Scully' and 'Road Rage' being sung by Patagonia, or maybe that was just my crap hearing. What we can really look forward to in the Fan Zone is a rousing rendition of 'River Plate Mountain High'.

Our prediction

Whilst fully aware that I've probably got at least six nations slated in for semi-final appearances, I feel Argentina should definitely be there too. The big occasion doesn't daunt them, and they've got the playmakers to make a difference when it counts.

....

Country: Iceland

Tournament history

World Cup virgins in 2018, and we can't wait to see them. It all seems to have come in a huge rush, with their quarter-final appearance at Euro 2016, on the road to which they beat someone or other in the Round of 16. This apparent Johnny-come-lately status does, however, mask an astonishing level of skill and organisation from a nation so small, and anyone belittling their chances over 90 minutes does so at their peril.

Is there a national league?

Yes, it's a well organised pyramid structure, with the top flight a 12-team affair called the Úrvalsdeild Karla. Understandably, most of the main Icelandic players are dotted around the European leagues, but four individuals from recent national squads play for clubs in their home nation. 150,000 Icelandic men, 25,000 between the ages of 18 and 35, 12,000 like football, 1,000 have any aptitude at all, 900 of those have day jobs. It's a struggle just to put out a squad and they beat England!!!

Manager / Coach

Heimir Hallgrímsson now has sole charge of the team, after his buddy and former co-coach Lars Lagerbäck moved to the Norwegian gig. His name still means Homely Son of Stone Helmet, much as it did at the time of Euro 2016, and he's still a dentist when he's not in his tracksuit.

Will they be doing that clapping thing?

William Hill has stopped taking bets.

Glancing through recent squad lists, is there any player whose surname doesn't end in either '-son' or '-sson'? I could do with some reassurance

Relax: there's a fair chance Frederik Schram will be selected as one of the squad's three goalkeepers.

Players to watch

Now that Eiður Guðjohnsen is off the scene, all eyes of fans of the curly 'd' style letter are on Everton's Gylfi Sigurðsson. Except for those that are on Jón Daði Böðvarsson, who is our outside bet for a clutch of memorable goals in the tournament, as well as boasting an impressive array of hieroglyphics on top of his name.

The word on the street

In a previous book, I dissed the Icelandic guy (Kris) who confidently predicted that his side would reach the quarter-finals, and look what happened. This time, I got hold of the same fella and he sees no reason to suggest they'll fare any worse at the World Cup this summer. Idiot!

Player lookalikes

The entire squad are either tanned, blond members of a range of boy bands or, in cases such as Birkir Bjarnason, minor members of Nirvana. Either way, they've got the music in them.

Player anagrams

I'm struggling to finish off quite a few anagrams here, as I end up having S, O and N left over. Any ideas? OK...

Ari Skúlason = O, UR a Lanki Ass

Böðvar Böðvarsson = Dr Mounted Bung Lass

Songs to sing in the Fan Zone

'Ice Ice Baby' and 'Baby It's Cold Outside' are obvious starters, to be followed by a main course of 'Glacier Eyes' by Radiohead and Joan Baez's 'Gullfoss Winds'. As to more modern stuff, all we can manage is Katy Perry's 'If You Can Afjord Me', so we're probably best off avoiding the communal singing and sticking to the clapping thing.

Our prediction

They'll get hammered by Argentina, but will see off Nigeria and Croatia to progress, before meeting their demise in the Round of 16. We'd love to see them go further again, but just feel it won't happen this time. (Co-author is going with Argentina and Croatia, the latter despite Dejan Lovren's worst efforts).

....

Country: Croatia

Tournament history

We all recall their 1998 heroics, when they came third in that year's World Cup, but things have been a lot quieter (and a lot more Davor Šuker-less) since. In Euro terms, there's been a mixed bag recently of group-stage exits and unimpressive Round of 16 forays.

Manager / Coach

Zlatko Dalić, who has lurked on the fringes of Hollywood as a stand-by extra in the 'Generic Latin Lover' role, is at the helm of his national squad, having managed in the UAE, Albania and Saudi Arabia earlier in his coaching career. Other than that, not much is known about him. Maybe he'll moon or engage in some other memorable act during the last group game.

Players to watch

Little to report in English Premier League terms, though Liverpool's Dejan Lovren can be relied upon to steady the ship at the back. (LOL! - Ed). Mario Mandžukić is still the man to provide the firepower up-front, but keep an eye on Modrić, Perišić and Rakitić chipping in from midfield.

The word on the street

Uniformly down-to-earth. There's no sense of any real optimism among the fans we contacted, who are all working on the assumption that Argentina are too strong and Iceland in too good form. There are rumours of points to be had in the Nigeria game, though.

Player lookalikes

Nikola Vlašić joins a maverick network of players from across FIFA's broad reach who are qualified to stand in for comedian/presenter Iain Lee. How this happened we have no idea – we just report it. In other news, Nikola Kalinić has now emerged unscathed from his Pat Nevin stage, and is actively seeking a new image.

Player anagrams

Luka Modrić as 'Dick L'Amour' went down (so to speak) very well at Euro 2016, so we're wheeling him out now for an encore. He is ably abetted by:

Ante Rebić = Beer? I Can't

Mato Miloš = O Mam, I Lost

Fran Tudor = O Fart Nurd

Lovro Majer = Major Lover

Songs to sing in the Fan Zone

For teeny-boppers, there's One Direction's 'Istria' to kick things off, followed by a good number of songs by The Sisak Sisters. More introspective 80s listening is provided by the work of Zadar Café and Split Enz, before Dire Straits round things off with a lively version of 'Twisting by the Pula'.

Our prediction

Group-stage exit. (Or not)

....

Country: Nigeria

Tournament history

The Super Eagles swooped to get their World Cup act together in 1994, and have qualified for most tournaments since, never really matching their potential or their nation's hopes. They won the Africa Cup of Nations in 2013, but then failed to qualify for the next two editions. All very puzzling.

Manager / Coach

German coach Gernot Rohr has the look of any one of 300 or so of Donald Trump's special advisers. He coached widely at club level across the French-speaking world, and is now onto his fourth African national team, after stints in Gabon, Niger and Burkina Faso. He hasn't got an obvious lookalike, but if I think of one I'll let you know.

Players to watch

A small number of squad members ply their trade in the English Premier League and Championship, but the bulk of recent squads is based in their home nation. Goal-scoring duties should fall to Ahmed Musa up-front and Victor Moses and Rabiu Ali contributing from midfield.

The word on the street

Realism is key here. Conversations centred on the unlikelihood of progressing, but also the opportunity to party and allow the younger players to shine in front of a worldwide audience.

So who are the cool pissers?

We're pinning our hopes on Kenneth Omeruo, Shehu Abdullahi, Ola Aina and Chidozie Awaziem to combine street swagger, savvy hair and general coolness in their approach to matters both football and media.

Player anagrams

Carl Ikeme = Cream-Like

Leon Balogun = Olé! A long Bun!

Kingsley Madu = Ye Mad Sulking

Moses Simon = Messi's Moon

Ahmed Musa = Sam Had Emu

Songs to sing in the Fan Zone

Kate Bush's 'Babooshka' lends itself well to being rewritten as 'Abuja', but only if we're pissed and slurring uncontrollably. In heavier terms, Iron Maiden's 'Kano Play with Madness' should rock the gaff, as well as triggering the response: 'I don't know; you'll have to ask Suggs about his recruitment policy'. Sam Smith's lilting 'Lagos Me Down' will bring everyone together for a smooch at the end.

Our prediction

Falling at the first hurdle, alas.

....

Group E

Country: Brazil

Tournament history

They've won the World Cup more times than Plymouth Argyle (you heard it here first), and their pedigree is proven, but interestingly they haven't triumphed in this competition since 2002. Equally baffling is their recent Confederations Cup record: they won it in 2013 but failed to qualify in 2017. It's been 11 years since they last won the Copa América. Most tellingly of all, they've never qualified for the Euros, so there's always a glimmer of hope. As the TV people start putting together their montage of flicks, tricks, free-kicks and scantily-clad rich Brazilian ladies, remember that Roberto Carlos only got that free kick right once, and on occasion Brazil is the dirtiest team in the world.[1]

Manager / Coach

Tite, a low-budget Grouty from *Porridge*, has a sparkling CV across a range of clubs in Brazil and the Middle East, though the Brazil national team is his first international appointment.

Players to watch

Take your pick. For obvious reasons, the spotlight will be on Neymar, but who's to argue against his branding, his proven ability

---

[1] Proof: https://www.youtube.com/watch?v=cfuD282WiWM There are 16 sendings-off in this clip (nine Brazilian) but the 1974 ref only gave one of them. How much did the Germans pay the Brazilians to do this to Holland? It's a question I urge you not to take seriously

and his international goal-scoring record (53 in 83 games, at the time of writing)?

Is there a Premier League rule that states that Brazilian internationals these days are only allowed to sign for Manchester City, Chelsea or Liverpool?

It certainly looks that way, yes.

The word on the street

Party, party party, and confidence of meeting either Argentina or Germany in the final. Nobody we spoke to could be shaken from this firm belief.

Player lookalikes

Thiago Silva is Jason Grimshaw from *Corrie*. Diego is a teasing amalgamation of Louis Tomlinson from One Direction and Xabi Alonso. David Luiz is that young lad out of Diversity, while the Scandinavian dimension (aided and abetted by judicious hair-dying) is provided by Lucas Lima.

Player anagrams

Taison = O Stain!

Casemiro = I'm Co-Arse

Marcelo = Leo Cram

Dani Alves = Dana Elvis

Ederson = Red Nose

Songs to sing in the Fan Zone

Duran Duran's 'Rio' is always a good place to start, fading effortlessly into Barry Manilow's 'Copacabana'. The late, great Kirsty MacColl makes a welcome reappearance with her rendition of 'Belém of Belfast City', and the party reaches its zenith with Take That's smoochy 'Brazilian Love Songs'.

Our prediction

Finalists – triumphant ones if they perform on the day. (Dissenting co-author strikes again!)

....

Country: Switzerland

Tournament history

Over the last generation or so, the Swiss have yo-yoed between group stage exits and last 16 progress in both the World Cup and the Euros, with no major breakthrough yet forthcoming. Their defence is sometimes as full of holes as a...no, can't think of the expression.

Manager / Coach

Vladimir Petković has been referred to as a 'Bosnian Father Ted', and recent pictorial evidence gives us no reason to deviate from that assertion. His club coaching experience – in Switzerland, Italy and Turkey – stood him in good stead to take over the Swiss national team four years ago, and his record so far isn't bad: he guided them to the Round of 16 in Euro 2016.

Switzerland's a nice, prosperous country, so presumably the entire squad is keen to live there and earn mega-bucks in the domestic Swiss league?

Au contraire. A glance at recent squads reveals no more than six players operating in the Swiss league.

Players to watch

LFB[2] Xherdan Shaqiri is still the man to watch, influencing play and chipping in with goals from midfield. Elsewhere, any other Swiss goals are likely to come from Eren Derdiyok and Haris Seferović.

I read somewhere that 'Djibril Sow plays with Young Boys'. Can you reassure me that nothing's amiss here?

Of course. Logic should tell you that Young Boys is a Swiss football club. If you'd read 'Djibril Boy plays with young sows', we'd be having a different conversation.

The word on the street

We encountered a lot of indifference among Swiss contacts, so much so that we're tempted to say they were remaining neutral. However, we did manage to tease out a modicum of self-belief in one fan (with a Portuguese surname), who wisely predicted that it may all hinge on the Serbia game: if they can get something there and beat Costa Rica, they ought to be OK.

Player lookalikes

Stephan Lichtsteiner is market inspector Robbie Jackson from *EastEnders* after acne-defeating facial reconstruction. When he

---

[2] Lovely fluent ball-player; what else could it be?

messes his hair up, Blerim Džemaili is transatlantic comedian Rich Hall. On the comedic theme, Admir Mehmedi is actually more familiar to us than we may realise, being defined as 'any Irish comedian you've never heard of, featuring on a dated re-run of *Live at the Apollo*'.

Player anagrams

Nico Elvedi = I'd Love Nice

Admir Mehmedi = Here I'm Mad, Dim

Gregor Kobel = Broke Logger

Fabian Frei = A Fani Brief

Valentin Stocker = Never Lacks Tinto

Songs to sing in the Fan Zone

We're starting funkily, with 80s groovers Linx offering up 'So This is Romansh', segueing into The Cure's 'Fribourg I'm in Love'. Rock fans are catered for by a comprehensive play-through of the Motorhead / Girlschool EP 'St Gallen-tine's Day Massacre', before the mood is mellowed by a welcome dip into the soundtrack from *The King and I*, with 'Whistle a Happy Thun'. (Did you do Ash's 'Berne Baby Berne' in the Euro 2016 book, then? –Ed. *Yep, afraid I did*.)

Our prediction

It's between the Swiss and the Serbians to scrape out of the group alongside Brazil. If you need an answer, we're going for Switzerland, on the grounds that we're less keen on Serbian chocolate and the mountain railways outside Belgrade aren't so impressive. (I don't see why he's writing off the Ticos so easily either.)

....

Country: Costa Rica

Tournament history

The mood is upbeat at present, following the nation's quarter-final appearance at the 2014 World Cup, where they lost to the Netherlands on penalties (or 'pelanties', as Chris Waddle put it at the time). They've performed steadily, if unremarkably, at CONCACAF level in recent years, and have won the lightly regarded Copa Centroamericana some eight times since 1991. (Well, if you're not going to mention that they beat Scotland at Italia 90 and England have never conceded a goal to them in a major competition, then I am. -Ed.)

Manager / Coach

Prior to landing the national coach role in his native Costa Rica, Óscar Ramírez was last seen in a pre-*Terry and June* BBC sitcom entitled *Moustachioed Executives in Crimplene Flares*, which unfortunately never got the green light after a disastrous pilot. He shook off that disappointment to forge a playing and coaching career, undertaken entirely in Costa Rica, most recently as national coach since 2015.

Costa Rica sounds very Hispanic, so you're going to tell me there's a 100% Spanish-sounding set of names making up the national squad, aren't you?

Yes, I can confirm it's 100% Latin-sounding. Apart from Patrick Pemberton, Rodney Wallace, Kendall Waston, Joel Campbell and Roy Miller. (Factual chip-in from co-author: probably descended from workers brought in from Jamaica to the west coast port of Limón once actual slavery had ceased; so still very much Costa

Rican, you'll find, although the Government didn't recognise Limón as part of the country until 1948.)

Who won the legendary 'unlucky dip' draw when the Christian names were handed out?

Well remembered. That was midfielder Yeltsin Tejada.

Players to watch

Joel Campbell is reasonably well known from his spell at parent club Arsenal, whence he was loaned out to Betis. He can still be dangerous, as can captain Bryan Ruiz, who single-handedly eliminated Italy from WC2014. The other Bryan (Oviedo) decided Sunderland would be a warmer and altogether more stimulating place to live than San José, so he made the move in 2017 after five years at Everton. Perhaps the standout talent is keeper Keylor Navas, who caught Real Madrid's eye at the last World Cup and has enjoyed considerable success since his move there.

The word on the street

Actually the word in the Costa Rican online press, if you'll forgive our reluctance to splash out £869 on a flight to San José via a baffling jigsaw of stopovers in the States, just to have a coffee and sample the mood. Midfielder Celso Borges turns out to be far more of a national favourite than you might have expected, and much is made of his ability to notch important goals from midfield. Borges aside, Navas as a safe pair of hands and the predatory combination of Ruiz and Campbell up-front dominate the headlines.

Player lookalikes

Kenner Gutiérrez was the surprise winner of Costa Rican TV's inaugural *Scandinavian Factor*, beating Francisco Calvo in a closely-fought flatpack-furniture-assembly play-off, while Danny Carvajal emerged triumphant from the simultaneously televised *Are You a Costa Rican Shay Given?* competition. Christian Bolaños is currently undergoing therapy to help him determine once and for all whether he's aiming for (a) the Ronaldinho look or (b) the Sharleen Spiteri vibe, or whether he should settle for an unhealthy amalgam of the two. Watch this space.

Player anagrams

Francisco Calvo = I Can Flavor Cocs

Deyver Vega = Every Veg Ad

Marvin Angulo = On Vaginal Rum

Heiner Mora = Ram Heroine

Songs to sing in the Fan Zone

It would be too obvious to start with 'Do You Know the Way to San José?', so we won't, preferring to go for The Lightning Seeds' 'Heredia or Not'. I'm sure you've all noticed that the city of Alajuela features repeatedly in the build-up to the lyric 'Tell me more, tell me more' in 'Summer Nights' from *Grease*. Otherwise we're reduced to evoking Don Henley's 'The Costa Living', spliced with Lil Wayne's 'Eu-Rica'.

Our prediction

Group-stage exit – sorry. (Hmmm...)

....

Country: Serbia

Tournament history

In both World Cup and European Championships terms, there's been a series of disappointments since the quarter-finals of Italia 90, however you care to define the Serbia / Montenegro / Yugoslavia nomenclature subtleties.

Manager / Coach

Mladen Krstajić's people are currently in discussions with Channel 4 Films about a possible role for Krstajić as a stunt-double for John Bishop in the latter's leading-actor romp in forthcoming blockbuster *Jeremy Kyle: The Movie*.

Players to watch

Of the England-based contingent, we're looking to Nemanja Matić and Dušan Tadić to make a degree of impact in midfield, with Aleksandar Mitrović poised to net a couple of beauties up-front (so keep him out of the Russian night-clubs). Former Chelsea hero Branislav Ivanović has now passed 100 caps for his country, and can still do a solid job in defence.

The word on the street

The girlfriend of someone I work with is Serbian, so she constitutes our sole expert in this section. In that role, I have to say she did an admirable job, informing us that Belgrade is a beautiful city, and that the country has some world-class spas. I pushed gently for a more football-based appraisal, and was rewarded with the news that her brother supports Partizan but he couldn't currently be reached for a comment as he was away on holiday in Croatia.

Player lookalikes

Keeper Vladimir Stojković refuses to accept that he's actor Ralph Ineson (Finchy from *The Office)* and, depending on the photo, he may have a point. Aleksandar Filipović has recovered well from his televised mishap in 2010, falling to his death in the guise of Bradley Branning in *EastEnders*. Adem Ljajić is either (or possibly both) of the blond lads from Westlife.

Player anagrams

Duško Tošić = Sock Studio

Dušan Tadić = A Nudist Cad

Zoran Tošić = Scot or Nazi?

Stefan Mitrović = Vice Farm – No Tits

Songs to sing in the Fan Zone

John Lennon's 'Serb Yourself' or Jack Conte's 'Make the Belgrade' could open the proceedings, but for real World Cup substance we need to turn to the timeless anthem 'Niš un Dorma', whose solemnity could then be followed by Bananarama's 'I Heard a Ruma' or the Oasis classic 'Sombor Might Say'. It's an uneasy mix, I grant you.

Our prediction

Group-stage exit, by a whisker and Dušan Tadić will look twice the player he does for Southampton.

....

Group F

Country: Germany

Tournament history

Now this gets tricky. Tell Lloyd Pettiford to look away for a moment, and I'll delight you with details of how well 'Germany' has done in the World Cup and the European Championship since 1934 and 1972 respectively. But the footballing histories of the previous East and West, and of the new unified Germany, are all well known, so to go easy on Lloyd's blood pressure I'll limit my input here to reminding our readers (both of you) that Germany won the World Cup in 2014, and that whilst they haven't won the Euros since 1996 in England, they have been finalists or semi-finalists in each of the last three editions of that competition.

Manager / Coach

We're delighted to welcome back Joachim 'Chachi off *Happy Days*' Löw for another round of ribald piss-taking based around what were referred to in a previous book as his 'famed nose-picking and resultant-snot-munching antics'.

Players to watch

Pretty much the same ones as we've admired and feared in equal measure over the last few tournaments. In terms of current form, it's probably worth pointing to Mats Hummels, Sami Khedira and Mario Götze, but in truth the Germans could put out any XI and still have a chance against the best. The enigmatic question this time around is: what kind of a tournament will Mesut Özil have? Miroslav Klose did finally retire, it's important to note.

The word on the street

I gathered together four German friends, bought them each a coffee and we joked for a while about national stereotypes. I then asked them about the forthcoming World Cup, and suggested they should give me a genuine opinion, rather than the kind of response I might be expecting as a result of the earlier banter about stereotypes. All four revealed a rock-solid certainty that Germany will win WC2018. Tick.

Player lookalikes

Previous German squads lacked the key Patrick Kielty role, but I'm happy to say that Bayer Leverkusen's Julian Brandt has stepped up and is poised to do all the required twinkly stuff in Russia. Sebastian Rudy has moonlighted seamlessly in recent years as Mathew Horne from *Gavin and Stacey*. Sandro Wagner gets through passport control pretty easily these days as a consummate Doppelgänger for 'Gary Windass from *Corrie* with his ginger hair dyed dark brown'.

Player anagrams

Sandro Wagner = Renown as Drag

Niklas Süle = Sulkin' Seal

Kevin Trapp = Krappin' Vet

Marcel Halstenberg = Smart Belle Changer

Songs to sing in the Fan Zone

Derived purely from players' names, we could offer The Beatles' 'Götze Get You Into My Life', Paul Young's 'Come Back and ter Stegen', The Specials' 'A Message to You, Rudy' and Abba's 'Kimmich, Kimmich, Kimmich (A Man After Midnight)', finishing off with us all linking arms and joining in a boisterous singalong of 'The Emre Can Can'.

Our prediction

Winners, unless they bottle it in the final. (Finalists. I cannot go to print believing Germany will win the World Cup – they'll go and put five stars on their shirts then, even though it was Westgermany, blah blah!)

....

Country: Mexico

Tournament history

Mexico have reached the quarter-finals of the World Cup twice, but not since 1986 and never outside Mexico. Nonetheless, having been banned in 1990 they finally got past the group stages outside Mexico in 1994. They repeated the feat in 1998, 2002, 2006, 2010 and 2014 but on each occasion lost in the round of 16. They made the semis of the Confederations Cup last year, and won the CONCACAF Gold Cup in 2015, the latest of ten triumphs in that (and its predecessor) championship. Pretty solid all round.

Manager / Coach

Juan Carlos Osorio is the result of an unfortunate cosmetic experiment back in 2003, in which Dustin Hoffman underwent a botched 'Hispanicisation' procedure in preparation for a role in a film that was eventually scrapped. A cheery consequence was that

Osorio has also become 'the future Ryan Giggs, circa 2034 vintage'. Every cloud.

Players to watch

It's Chicharito all the way - touching 30 despite the baby face, but on great form for West Ham and with (at the time of writing) 49 goals from 100 appearances for the national side. Other players expected to complement Hernández's goals are veteran striker Oribe Peralta and captain Andrés Guardado.

Can we have a token German-sounding squad member to reflect European migration trends of yesteryear, please?

OK, since you asked nicely: Jürgen Damm.

The word on the street

There's no weak team in this group, but the two Mexicans we spoke to were confident that their boys will have just enough to keep South Korea and Sweden at bay, to progress from the group with Germany. One of them joked that it's unnatural to be both Mexican and sure of something at the same time, but he was quietly confident that it'll all be OK in Russia.

Much store is set by trendiness of hair, but do any of the Mexican squad suffer from difficult-to-control or 'excitable' hair, I wonder idly?

Now that you come to mention it, Carlos Vela and Jonathan dos Santos both get through a fair bit of 'product'. Guillermo Ochoa takes us back to the glory days of the mad Latin American perm and, frankly, the tournament will be all the better for it.

Player anagrams

César Montes = Come, Rent Ass

Carlos Vela = Love Rascal

Omar Govea = A Grave Moo

Luis Montes = Muesli Tons

Rodrigo Salinas = Lasso a Ring-Roid

Songs to sing in the Fan Zone

We kick off on a nostalgic front, with Amy Winehouse's 'Someone to Ochoa Me', before upping the jiggy potential with ABC's 'Toluca Love' (acknowledging that this is also on offer under the guise of an even crapper pun in the Saudi Arabian Fan Zone) or The Beach Boys' eternal question 'Tijuana Dance?' We can then bring the party up to date with Rudimental's 'León It All On Me'. That should do it. It'll have to - I've run out of crap gags. (Can I just mention Wall of Voodoo's under-rated classic 'Mexican Radio' from 1982? Includes the never to be forgotten lyric 'wish I was in Tiajuana, eating barbequed iguana'.)

Our prediction

Impressive group stage, then curtains in the Round of 16 as usual.

....

Country: Sweden

Tournament history

Sweden were the World Cup runners-up in 1958, and reached the semis of the Euros in 1992. In the 2000/01 season, Sweden came fifth in the last-ever edition of the Nordic Football Championship. Fifth? Behind whom? And fifth out of how many? How big is the Nordic pool of countries, for Thor's sake? It turns out that if you count them all off on your fingers, including Iceland and the Faroe Islands, you get to six. The Faroes (with whom Sweden drew 0-0) finished sixth. Dark days indeed.

Manager / Coach

There will come a time when facial recognition software allows us to merge faces and make sections like this much more credible. However, back in 2018 (and please indulge me on this one): Janne Andersson often struggles to get through passport control without a Swedish official asking him (in Swedish, obvs): 'Are you verily the amalgam of Adrian Chiles and 1970s sex god Crystal Palace winger Peter Taylor, who went on to coach at national level?' Time after time – it must really get him down.

Players to watch

Some of the old guard, like Sebastian Larsson, Marcus Berg, Mikael Lustig and captain Andreas Granqvist are still around and capable of doing a job (if not necessarily professional football). Otherwise, it's likely to be a youthful squad that's entrusted to make the trip to Russia.

The gag about surnames ending with the same suffix has been done to death, so can you supply a potential squad member whose name might simply make us smile?

Fair enough. How about Simon Tibbling?

The word on the street

Zlatan Ibrahimović featured in every conversation I had about the Swedish team's chances – his are big boots to fill, for sure. The general word was that they should be able to take care of South Korea, and that the Mexican game will be the crunch one.

Player lookalikes

Victor Lindelöf is a young Emilio Butragueño, which bodes well for his footballing future (unlike being routinely left on the bench at Manchester United). Simon Tibbling has the look of a pre-pubescent train-spotter whose uncontrollable delight has gone through the roof on receiving an 'access all areas' pass to the National Railway Museum in York. No offence, mate. (He's unlikely to have a clue what you're on about – like the rest of us. -Ed.)

Player anagrams

Anton Tinnerholm = Not the Normal Inn

Andreas Linde = Lads Need Iran

Albin Ekdal = A Kinda Bell

Emil Krafth = Father Milk

Songs to sing in the Fan Zone

The Stranglers kick us off lustily with 'Sweden (All Quiet on the Eastern Front)', with The Clash continuing the robust punk theme with 'Lund-on Calling'. In fact, let's go punk (and inspired sub-genres) all the way and bring in Linköping Park for a guest appearance.

Our prediction

Will be squeezed out by Germany and Mexico in the group stage.

....

Country: South Korea

Tournament history

Nothing may ever beat the euphoria of South Korea reaching the semi-finals in 2002, in the World Cup they co-hosted with Japan. They're the current holders of the EAFF East Asian Cup, which may not have produced quite the same euphoria.

Manager / Coach

Shin Tae-yong is the world's leading John Noakes Hair-a-Like, which is an accolade he would wear with pride if he knew what it meant. His entire playing and coaching career has been based in South Korea, apart from a stint in Australia, where expats of a certain age knew who John Noakes was and gave him odd looks from time to time. He's progressed rapidly through the ranks at national level, and has been head cheese since 2017.

Players to watch

There's a high concentration of home-based talent in the South Korean ranks, together with a good few playing in Japan and a handful in China. Interestingly, none of the current squad seems to be playing in the North Korean league. England-based players likely to get a game in Russia are Crystal Palace's Lee Chung-yong and Son Heung-min of Spurs, who has a tasty goal-scoring record. In this department, however, the main man remains Lee Dong-gook, who can be relied upon to notch a goal every three games (though his teammates might be urging him to up the ante a bit in the three-game group stage).

The word on the street

This is considerably easier to ascertain than would be the case north of the border. Our contacts still think there's a good chance of their nation getting out of the group, though are reluctant to be drawn on the likelihood of emulating the feats of 2002.

I'm on the lookout for some examples of edgily stylish South Korean hair, possibly with the optional addition of some coppery-bronze highlights. Can you help me?

You need more than the kind of help I can offer, mate. However, in answer to your question, look no further than goalkeeper Kim Seung-gyu and captain Jung Woo-young. More squad members are expected to jump on the bandwagon once they've read this book in the weeks leading up to the tournament.

Player anagrams

Any anagram aficionado seeking to make mischief with combinations of 'young dongs' and 'randy wangs' will be in heaven with the South Korean squad. However, to keep things clean, feast your eyes on the following:

Lee Dong-gook = Do Google Ken

Rim Chang-Woo = Ringo Cow Ham

Lee Chang-min = Leeching Man

Ju Se-jong = Jug Jones

Son Heung-min = Hi, Gnome Nuns!

Songs to sing in the Fan Zone

Back to The Clash to fire in with 'Korea Opportunities', before the mood gets steamier with any of a dozen versions of 'Seoul Man'. The soul vibe continues with Erma Franklin's 'Daegu Nother Little Piece of My Heart', before the dance floor erupts with a dance-along rendition of 'Gangnam Style'. We asked Psy to sponsor this section in return for a name-check of his song, but his people told us to feck off. As part of the ongoing cordial north-south relations (in which Koreans marched together in the winter Olympic opening ceremony, both realising now that it's actually Trump who's the threat) we agreed to throw in Kim Wilde's entire back catalogue into this section.

Our prediction

Group-stage exit. Tears and respectfully controlled tantrums.

....

Group G

Country: Belgium

Tournament history

Quarter-finals in both World Cup 2014 and Euro 2016, despite the unquestionable quality of both squads. Is something missing? The new coach could be the man to put this right.

Is there any relationship between the 'Belgian waffle' in culinary terms and the same expression in respect of the drafting of World Cup books? They both seem difficult to digest.

Very astute of you. I aim to please.

Manager / Coach

Roberto Martínez is well known in the English divisions, as a stylish player, occasionally tactically astute coach and all-round nice guy. The less well known side of his personal life is revealed in his anagram 'Mr Nitrate Boozer'. Whatever gets you through training sessions, I suppose.

Players to watch

Quite simply, the Belgian squad (very stable across recent call-ups, incidentally, which cannot be said of the majority of sides disputing WC2018) has an embarrassment of riches, with nearly 50% of them on the books of clubs in the English leagues (plus Dedryck Boyata leading the 'mad hair' initiative at Celtic). To pick out any individuals would be the stuff of folly, so a-follying I will go, with the unsurprising 'keep an eye on Hazard, De Bruyne and Lukaku'.

The word on the street

Plenty of it (served with chips and mayonnaise). Both the fans we spoke to agreed with us that 2018 will be the year when their boys finally do themselves justice and get to the semis.

Player lookalikes

Radja Nainggolan is a very busy man, combining his role as Roma midfielder, deputy bass-player with any band looking or sounding like The Exploited, and a burgeoning celebrity berth as 'an even angrier-looking John Terry'. Yannick Carrasco may think he's got us fooled with the flimsy beard disguise, but we all know he's Jamie Theakston. Gary Lineker is widely reported as having four sons, but the addition of Adnan Januzaj as Number Five is less commonly known (and palpably untrue, we hasten to add for legal reasons).

Player anagrams

Simon Mignolet = Sing Me Moonlit

Thomas Meunier = Tram in Me House

Thomas Foket = Most Hot Fake

Yannick Carrasco = Carry Sock in a Can

Songs to sing in the Fan Zone

What better place to start than 'Chanson Namur'? Probably plenty of places... Step forward The Pretenders with 'Aalst Stand by You'. The back catalogue of Uriah Ypres is worth exploring, as is that of

David Hasselt-Hof, by which time we're ready for a throaty all-together-now of Robbie Williams's seminal 'Let Me Genkertain You' and Abba's timeless 'Waterloo'.

Our prediction

Huge potential, but possibly not quite the finished article. Semis.

....

Country: Panama

Does Panama feature in any famously lengthy palindromes?

Yes, thanks for asking: 'a man, a plan, a canal, Panama' usually does the trick.

Fair enough. But can they play football?

See below.

How does the national league shape up?

It's, shall we say, modest, in both its quality and its aspirations. In the current national squad, only three Panamanian clubs are represented: Chorrillo ('Little Jet'), Tauro ('Taurus') and Árabe Unido ('United Arab'). Make of that what you will. In 2017, two of the ten top-tier teams used the national team's training pitch (spectator capacity: 900) as their home ground.

Tournament history

Panama are World Cup Finals virgins, and it's great to see them qualify after a near-miss in 2014. They have a decent recent history in both the Copa Centroamericana and the CONCACAF Gold Cup.

Manager / Coach

Colombian Hernán Darío Gómez shook off the effects of an incident in which he was reported to have attacked a woman while manager of his native country's national team, and has been in charge in Panama since 2014. Facially, he is often held up by Newcastle NHS Trust as a stark warning to TV architect George Clarke to 'go easy on the pies'

Players to watch

With squad members dotted around Central and South America, Eastern Europe, the USA and the third tier of the Spanish league, it's difficult for them to get together frequently for a kick-about and a bit of tactical work with boss-man Gómez. Fans of nationally inappropriate surnames will note with glee that recent Panamanian squads have included a Davis, a Stephens, a Cooper, a Hughes, a Miller, a Dixon, a Cummings, a Nurse, a Clarke, a Taylor, a Blackburn and two Smalls. A cloud of doom hangs over the historically unfortunate surname of defender Fidel Escobar. Anyway, Guatemala-based veteran striker Blas Pérez is your man for goal-scoring prowess, ably assisted by Luis Tejada, who plies his trade in Peru.

The word on the street

The only people we managed to contact were Americans of Panamanian descent, who were unanimous in stating that they're unlikely to get anything out of the group games against Belgium and England, and are going to focus simply on enjoying the experience. Wise words.

Any mad haircuts I can look out for?

We're pinning our hopes on Aníbal Godoy (a) being selected and

(b) continuing his fruitful sequence of impressive tall-standing barnets. With or without bleaching, his coiffure rules the roost in the Panamanian ranks. Rolando Blackburn does his best to follow suit but, despite being a year older than Godoy, lacks experience in this department.

Player anagrams

Aníbal Godoy = On a big lady O!

Roberto Nurse – No Trebor user

Edgar Bárcenas = Sage Bra Dancer

Songs to sing in the Fan Zone

Aside from the obvious (but little known) 'Panama' by Van Halen, we're struggling. Pushing out from the capital into secondary cities, we would perhaps go for anything by Boquete and the MGs, Joe Cocle or Ocu-la Shaker; Dexy's 'Colón Eileen', the all-time classic 'Sona va Preacherman' or 'Santiago's Coming to Town' might get people's feet tapping, but would be unlikely to make them laugh. Singing 'There's Only One Panamanian' to famous Cuban song 'Guantanamera' may be fairly pointless when faced with a squad of 23, but it fits well.

Our prediction

Group stage performances likely to be dubbed 'plucky' by most of the Anglophone press, but little chance against such strong opposition. (England can lose to anyone, though! -Ed)

....

Country: Tunisia

Tournament history

'The Eagles of Carthage' have qualified for the World Cup Finals on four previous occasions, but have yet to get out of the group, winning only one game in total (a 3-1 defeat of Mexico in 1978 in Argentina). Their main international success has come elsewhere, winning the Africa Cup of Nations in 2004 and the confusingly named, but different, African Nations Championship in 2011.

Can we expect any 'tasty' friction between Tunisia and Morocco?

No, for two reasons. Politically, they're good mates, and footballistically, neither is likely to get out of the group stage, so a meeting on the pitch in Russia ain't gonna happen.

Manager / Coach

Depending on the direction of the wind, Nabil Maâloul is either the unacknowledged cousin of the much-missed Barry Evans from *EastEnders* or the guy who came second to Gennaro Contaldo in Jamie Oliver's *Search for an Italian Chef to accompany me on all my TV shows Factor.*

Who won the recent 'least Tunisian-sounding name in the squad' competition?

Ah, yes – that was Dylan Bronn.

Players to watch

Veteran goalkeeper and captain Aymen Mathlouthi is, on his day, as safe a pair of hands as you'd hope for, but he's not always on his day. Syam Ben Youssef provides defensive rigidity as well as an appropriately thuggish look. Elsewhere, keep an eye out for goal-scoring midfielder Wahbi Khazri, who plays for Rennes and boasts a seriously cheeky grin.

The word on the street

Tunisians are thin on the ground in the Yorkshire village where I live, so this section is based on gleaning what I could from the Francophone press. This didn't amount to much, but there does seem to be a sense of grim realism, knowing that Belgium and England await Tunisia in the group.

Player lookalikes

Ali Maâloul is any minor member of popsters The Feeling in their more mature, introspective (and hence beard-sporting) phase. Khalil Chemmam is blissfully unaware of this, but his great-uncle twice-removed is none other than 70s sitcom staple George Layton. Wouldn't we all like to have that on our CV? Youssef Msakni has made no secret of his desire to be the Tunisian Neymar, and he's made good strides in this quest, but the current grading is 'C+, more work needed'.

Player anagrams

Anice Badri = C.I.A. Brained

Naïm Sliti = A Sin Limit

Aymen Trabelsi = My Rabelais Net / Tries Ably, Amen

Bassem Srarfi = Firm Arse Bass

Songs to sing in the Fan Zone

There's Roxette's beautiful 'June(isia) Afternoon', of course, followed by 'Chew(nisia)bacca' by Supernova. If that's not enough – which I can confirm it isn't – you could look to work by Aryanah Grande or perhaps Eminem's 'Kef-ful What You Wish For'.

Our prediction

It all hinges on whether Joe Hart drops any crucial crosses and lets Tunisia in through the back door. On balance, we're going for Belgium and England to progress from the group, leaving Tunisia tantalisingly close but ultimately disappointed.

....

Country: England

Tournament history

Ee-aye-addio, we won the cup. In 1966. That aside, lots of clichés about hurt and heartache, wrapped up in multiples of ten years.

Manager / Coach

Gareth Southgate was once described as Chris Coleman without access to a sunbed. In truth, he doesn't appear to have suffered too much in stress terms since taking the helm of the good ship England, and the squad he's assembled seems to be in good nick, but 2018 will obviously be a make-or-break year.

Players to watch

We know the main players inside out, so it's really a question of identifying who will rise to the occasion and who will flatter to deceive. More than ever, the scouts from the big continental European clubs will be Kane-spotting, but something tells us he's got the resilience now to continue to deliver under such scrutiny. Alongside him up-front, Vardy and Rashford can still produce the goods, but with Rooney now out of the way can we expect a blistering cameo from veteran Jermain Defoe? (No. -Ed.)

The word on the street

Very, very confident (too much so?). Prior to every tournament we wonder idly whether this will be the one, only for dreams to fizzle for the usual reasons. Is it time to dampen our expectations, or will 2018 really be the year? The fact that the failures of the past (semi- and quarter-finals) would now look like successes probably tells all.

Player lookalikes

Swerving previous analyses, we find ourselves drawn to whether Michael Keane passes the test for bearing a passing resemblance to 'any other footballing Keane we've ever come across (apart from Robbie)'? Tick. In other news, Harry Winks came home to Cheryl the other day with a takeaway and she didn't even notice that he wasn't the Liam Payne she was expecting. If you're concerned that Phil Jones might no longer look like a younger Louis Van Gaal, worry not: this box remains very much ticked.

Player anagrams

Luke Shaw = UK Whales

Harry Winks = Wary Shrink

Ruben Loftus-Cheek = UK Lose French Tube

Tom Heaton = Hot Man Toe

Songs to sing in the Fan Zone

The key to stirring up healthy national footballing fervour (and we know this from experience, having failed on numerous occasions in the past) is to identify a musical pun based on one's national stadium. Step forward 'Wembley Collide' by Biffy Clyro who, obligingly, (a) are Scottish and (b) look like a semi-deponent Welsh verb. If you'd like me to empty my 'kept in reserve' bag of bands and singers sounding like potential (at the time of writing) squad-member surnames, fill your boots with Hart, Gunn, The Walker Brothers, The Rolling Stones, Axl Rose, Plastic Bertrand, Keane, Gomez, Dier Straits, Father Abraham, Patsy Clyne, Gnarls Barkley and The Kane Gang.

Our prediction

You know what? I'm going to go out on a limb here and say that England will perform admirably, albeit with a couple of wobbles, in their group, then will come undone in the knockout stages. I know: radical.

....

Group H

Country: Poland

Tournament history

In World Cup terms, things have been quiet in the Polish camp since a brace of third places in 1974 and 1982. Their quarter-final appearance in Euro 2016 may be more significant as an indicator of contemporary form.

Manager / Coach

Adam Nawałka is still in change, his stock now high after a relatively successful Euro 2016. If you narrow your eyes and glance at him from a distance of 50 yards or so, there is an element of Sean Bean in his smile. He's still tentative about crossing out the L in his surname more boldly, but the Polish Federation have lined up some assertiveness training for him pre-tournament.

Players to watch

It's hard to believe that Robert Lewandowski is still in his 20s – he seems to have been firing the goals in for Bayern and for the national side for as long as we can remember (which, in my case, isn't very long these days). At the risk of stating the obvious, he's still the main threat up-front, with useful goal contributions likely to come from Jakub Błaszczykowski and Arkadiusz Milik. In terms of English-league involvement, fans of QPR, Palace, Hull City, Bournemouth and West Brom may have one eye on Poland's progress, and Lloyd Pettiford will paint a convincing portrait of the merits of Southampton's Jan Bednarek. (Never heard of him!)

The word on the street

Conversations centred on the buoyancy triggered by Euro 2016, and tended towards the strength of the squad and a certain optimism that they'll be able to go one better this time and get to the semis.

Player lookalikes

Artur Boruc has recently moved away from Shay Given territory and is evolving quietly into a passable Ronan Keating. Kamil Grosicki has grudgingly accepted that his English isn't yet good enough for him to deputise on set for *Coronation Street's* Steve McDonald, but the camera crew told me he handles the long-shots with some aplomb (unlike Artur Boruc). Meanwhile, Grzegorz Krychowiak has been spotted consulting with his twin Greg Rusedski about how to handle life outside sport.

Player anagrams

Thiago Cionek = A Thickie Goon

Maciej Rybus = Juicy Breams

Maciej Sadlok = O Sick Jam Deal

Would it help if there were fewer Zs, Js and Ws in Polish names = Yes

Songs to sing in the Fan Zone

It is anticipated that the Polish Fan Zone will replicate the music being listened to by the national squad through their expensive headphones, all of which is by artists reflecting their own names. Narcissistic buggers. We can therefore expect to encounter work by Milik Vanilli, Sadlok Café, Basement Jach and Steppen-Wolski.

This sequence will be bookended by the timeless classics 'Kamil Chameleon' and 'Peszko Round Again', while more cerebral readers may be enticed by the prospect of listening to an audio-book recording of Ian Rankin narrating his *Inspector Rybus* mysteries in Polish. Heady stuff.

Our prediction

Last 16 – no further.

....

Country: Senegal

Tournament history

The Lions of Teranga memorably got to the quarter-finals in WC2002, where they were heartbreakingly squeezed out by Turkey after extra time and cheating. They were runners-up in the Africa Cup of Nations the same year, but pickings since then have been slim. It's great to see them back at the finals.

Manager / Coach

Aliou Cissé is the man in change. Little is known about the coaching prowess of Cissé, who is remembered more on these shores for his playing career at Portsmouth and Birmingham. To his credit, though, his side currently looks well organised and full of flair.

Players to watch

There's a good sprinkling of England-based players in the Senegalese ranks, perhaps most notably Sadio Mané at Liverpool.

His partnership up-front with either Moussa Sow or Mame Diouf looks set to be key.

Is Sow the only forward in the squad whose surname is both a female animal and an English verb?

As far as I can see he's unique in that respect, yes.

The word on the street

Difficult to judge in terms of direct quotes taken from the streets of Dakar, but we managed to track down a French exchange student of Senegalese descent, who was pretty clued up on the current squad and the road to qualification. He told us that the national press is going mad for Mané, and that expectations of getting through the group are running high. His own view was that they should get past Japan, then we'll have to wait and see. Indeed so.

Presumably the Senegalese side are top of the pile in artistic hairstyle deployment?

Yes, there are jauntily mad crops throughout the squad, from Alfred Gomis in goal though Kara Mbodji and Adama Mbengue in defence, to Lamine Gassama and Alfred N'Diaye in midfield, ably supported by M'Baye Niang up-front. Unfortunately, a lot of the lads didn't get the memo, and habitually sport the low-maintenance number-one-all-over. This is all very well for ease of pre- and post-match grooming, but frankly, on the World Cup stage, we expect better.

Player anagrams

Sadio Mané = A Mad Noise

Alfred N'Diaye = Already Fined

Salif Sané = Fine Salsa

Clément Diop = Complete Din

Alfred Gomis = Mailed Frogs

Fallou Diagne = Led Foul Again

Songs to sing in the Fan Zone

There's 'Senegal' by Blink 182 and 'Begin the Pikine' by Julio Iglesias, of course, but most Senegalese fans assembled in Russia will be belting out The Seekers' 'Dakar-nival is Over'. It's what they do, and we need to respect that.

Our prediction

Lots of style, lots of flair, lots of smiles, but very few goals, and a group-stage exit.

....

Country: Colombia

Tournament history

Not great through history (excepting an impressive Copa América triumph in 2001), but similar to group-mates Poland, they have recent quarter-final pedigree, having reached that stage in the 2014 World Cup, where they were edged out 2-1 by hosts Brazil. Seemed like a great result until Brazil lost their next two matches by an aggregate of 1-10.

Manager / Coach

Depending on the angle of the stalker's zoom lens, José Pékerman is either a wizened Richie Benaud or a latter-day version of *Just Good Friends* actor Paul Nicholas. Quite a bit of variation for you to chew over there, but where all commentators agree is on his status as the possessor of the funniest surname among the WC2018 coaching fraternity (though presumably it's not quite so funny in the original Ukrainian). Either way, Argentine native Pékerman has established good coaching credentials during his six years at the Colombian helm.

Players to watch

Oh, for the glory days of Carlos Valderrama, René Higuita and their superlative barnets. These days we're stuck with less flamboyant stars (though pretty impressive as footballers, we should say in fairness). David Ospina at Arsenal, José Izquierdo at Brighton and Davinson Sánchez at Tottenham are the key British-based players, but inevitably all eyes will be on James Rodríguez to justify (a) the hype and (b) his inexplicably Anglo-Saxon first name and its even more inexplicable phonetic butchering by the Spanish-speaking media. 'Ham-ez' aside, goals could come from a number of sources, but we're looking to Carlos 'Chew' Bacca and Radamel 'Rock Me Amadeus' Falcao to vindicate our faith and bang a few in.

The word on the street

Actually very modest. We spoke by Skype to one Colombian fan, whose view was that the country is pretty realistic about its chances this time – no major Latin hyperbole or anything. Disappointing.

Player lookalikes

If we could be teleported back to the aforementioned glory days, we'd be having fun here with stuff about early regency coiffures, 'blond Fellainis' and so on. However, we can only work with the squad we've got, so logically we start by heading to *Corrie* to check out Carlos Bacca's recent subscription to the burgeoning Jason Grimshaw club. On his 18th birthday, Santiago Arias told his family he was setting out on a quest to become Chandler from *Friends*, but eight years on he still hasn't quite nailed it.

Player anagrams

Pablo Armero = A Poor Ambler

Daniel Torres = Soiled Errant

Felipe Pardo = O Dapper Life!

Avilés Hurtado = Valid House Art

Mateus Uribe = I Rub E.U. Mates

Stefan Medina = Mated Fannies

Songs to sing in the Fan Zone

Anything on Colombia Records would be appreciated, but given the spelling anomaly we'd need to look to artists like Bogotá and the MGs, Cali Minogue, Doctor and the Medellíns and Cartagena the Unstoppable Sex Machine. Equally, we could pay homage to squad members with tracks like the Steve Miller Band's 'Fabracadabra', Take That's 'Bacca for Good' or Bill Withers' 'Moreno Sunshine'. Anyone still pining for scorpion-kicking goalkeeping antics of yesteryear will be catered for by Elton John's 'Higuita' on a loop. (Or 'Chick-Higuita' by Abba?)

Our prediction

This is a tough one. In theory, they should have enough to get through the group, but something tells me Japan are going to play out of their skins and pip them to the post.

....

Country: Japan

Tournament history

In recent World Cup history, Japan have hop-scotched between group-stage exits and Round of 16 disappointments. They've won the AFC Asian Cup four times (most recently in 2011), and lost to France in the final of the 2001 Confederations Cup. Overall, it's baffling that they haven't achieved wider success, given their acknowledged discipline, fitness and tactical improvement in the last generation or so.

Manager / Coach

Bosnian Vahid Halilhodžić is a genetically-modified amalgam of seven or eight international coaches we've known and loved (or hated) since about 1990. The DIY aspect of this feature is for you to add faces of your choice into the mix, and I'm sure you'll be better at it than I am. With Halilhodžić, it's all about figures. He scores a respectable two bonus points for the 'mad hieroglyphics above surname' factor, and has had coaching experience with an astonishing 82% of all clubs registered worldwide, as well as an impressive 53% of the national sides. (No idea what you're on about?! –Ed.)

How's the J-League faring these days?

It's booming, with massive finances and advertising revenue and plenty of exposure. The bulk of the established members of the national squad still play in the top (J-1) league, though quite a lot of recently called up players ply their trade across Europe. It's fair to say that the J-League is going from strength to strength, and has a good future ahead of it.

Players to watch

Not currently too much UK-based involvement, other than Southampton's Maya Yoshida and Shinji Okazaki at Leicester City. The latter is, by some distance, his national team's leading scorer, but we can also expect goals from midfield from the prolific Shinji Kagawa and Keisuke Honda.

Are all the big motorcycling brands represented in the squad?

Good question. Bit of a mixed bag, since you ask. Keisuke Honda's certainly involved, and we have a clutch of near-misses with Shūto Yamamoto, Hotaru Yamaguchi and Mū Kanazaki rattling the crossbar.

The word on the street

Polite, respectful and diffident. I asked one Japanese guy in Nottingham, who chuckled and said that it would be nice to dream, but it ain't gonna happen this time.

I'm interested in the meaning of Japanese characters. Please can you make up some bollocks by way of a transliteration of the names of a few squad members?

Sure. Happy to oblige if you're sure that's what you want. Here we go with some literal meanings, which will necessarily sound clunky as they mirror the character-by-character progression of the original Japanese:

Eiji Kawashima (GK) = Spiky-furred four-limbed dragon isolated between sticks

Maya Yoshida (DF) = Industrious rampart drawn mercenarily to coast of the south

Shinji Kagawa (MF) = Faintly-recalled workhorse in guise of red devilled bench-warmer

Shinji Okazaki (FW) = Wily lank-tressed, Alice-banded Vardy out-doer

Player anagrams

Wataru Endo = War on a Duet

Ryota Morioka = Roy Took Maria

Masato Morishige = Moist Gash? O Marie!

Songs to sing in the Fan Zone

This is an open goal at national level, with classics like The Vapors' 'Turning Japanese', Aneka's 'Japanese Boy', Alphaville's 'Big in Japan' and so on. Sorry? What's that? Oh, you don't want the factual, you want the bollocks? Right you are: The Scissor Sisters' 'Tokyo Mama';

Phil Collins doing 'A Groovy Hokkaido Love'; Alanis Morissette chipping in with 'Kyoto Know'; Imagine Dragons' 'Osaka for Pain', Fleetwood Mac's 'Nagoya Own Way' and so on. Well, you did ask.

Our prediction

Japan will scrape through the group (after what might be described as a Nippon Tuck race to the line) but they'll get hammered in the Round of 16. As will I, on gallons of red wine. Goodnight.

....

You're Not Singing Anymore

A section mostly about teams who failed to qualify and how they feel about it... although starting with one who did, but probably won't take it seriously until they're 3-0 up in the final and who will absolutely refuse to get enthusiastic about it like the rest of us.

A View from FRANCE: Ambiguous Support at All Times[1]

There is a scene in Monty Python's *Holy Grail* where John Cleese plays the part of a French taunter...you remember? All that 'father was a hamster, mother smelled of elderberries' nonsense. Well you English all think that is funny because of the outrageous French accent, right? And the Germans think it's funny because Cleese calls for *la vache* and a catapult launches a cow at the silly English K-nigg-etts. Well, let me tell you that from the other side of *La Manche*, it's not funny at all. It's how things are. It's how we see you.

In fact, you bloody roast-beefs think everything is so bloody funny, don't you? Well, it's not. Always irritating us with your so-called 'self-deprecation' and then going bananas over your inadequate football team. Self-deprecation only works if you are not already

---

[1]   Based on original idea by Peter Wilkin who lives in France.

merde in the first place. And believe me you're super-*merde*. Yes, all of you. And especially your team.

You think we have no comedians in France, but that's only because we don't need them. We spend all our time laughing at you! Your lack of self-control around alcohol, your schoolboy-standard football team and, most of all, your politicians. Nigel Farage? Pah! Do you know what *farager* means in French? Absolutely nothing... but it should mean to be a stupid f***er who f***s everything up big style. And as for Theresa May...Theresa may what? May be a stupid f***er who f***s everything up big style! It's like the bloody Southampton FC youth academy except for right-wing idiots rather than footballers. One after the other they come rolling off the production line – pig f***kers, buffoons, upper-class imbeciles; all intent on national self-mutilation. What could be funnier? For us.

I'm sorry if this offends your sensibilities, but really you are all 'jolly amusants'. Especially this getting behind your team no matter what...now, what is *that* all about? Much better to shrug your shoulders, pretend you don't care and that what really matters in life are fashion, philosophy, impenetrable cinema and cuisine (and no, curry powder and chips are not the basis of a 'cuisine'). You can always get behind the team in the final few metres and, of course, disown them if they fail. But unequivocal support? That would be very un-French.

So I do not care who wins this bloody World Cup. Your papers will be full of insane optimism and using pointless military metaphors like the 'Dunkirk spirit'. As if that's relevant - you all ran away! But, anyway, it's been over 200 years now since France had an interest in Russia and that won't be changing. Unless we reach the semis, of course. And *les Anglais?* Already I can hear the bleating of a guilt-ridden Chris Waddle as you exit after a goalless draw with Iran or Panama. *Allez les Bleus. Peut-être.*

A View from North America 1: US of A: Simply the Best

Soccer is simply the best! Just like the USA. Wow, if Donald isn't just making the country grate again and we love 'foot-the-ball' – as you guys call it – more than anything. Well after NFL, NBA and baseball, obviously. Oh, and ice hockey for those wannabe Canadians in Minnesota. And tennis, lacrosse and track and field. Oh and eating, we like that more too. And shooting each other. But really, we have all just loved soccer since we held the inaugural World Cup of 1994. Of course we didn't actually invent football, like Christopher Columbus didn't discover the Americas, but it didn't really exist before then; not properly because we didn't care about it.

And then in 1994 all our Mexicans, Bolivians, Greeks, Italians and Poles, they all suddenly got excited and I thought 'how can anyone be interested in a sport which doesn't have breaks to sell you something?' Hell, that's downright un-American! And where you have a zero-zero tie at least half the time and *always* at half-time? When do we get to whoop and high-five, I ask ya! All seemed a bit communist to me. But I must say (loudly, obviously), over time I've come to appreciate the subtleties, like when the umpire really likes a guy he waves a red card at him and gets him to wait in his changing room for him. That's proper equality. And wow! – The thrill we get when the ball breaks the plane of the netted end-zone. Now that's special.

My favourite English player is that Dan Rooney...no, no, Wayne Rooney, is it? He's got great hustle, releases the wide areas for outside plays into the penalty zone and really makes the UK team tick. He may not be everyone's 'saucer of milk' (as I think you say) but with so many Hollywood stars looking perfect, it's refreshing that you have a hero who could have been in *Shrek*. Wow, I'm hearing he actually was in *Shrek*. That's just marvellous. Anyway, I can't wait for the next World Cup to start; then we'll be able to tell who the *real* patriots are, and in Trumpville, USA that may be just the kind of platinum intel we need. God bless us all. Us, not you. Whaddya mean we didn't qualify? Stupid Limey game anyways.

A View from North America 2: Canada: Simply the Best (at Hockey – Ice Variety)

Well, we didn't qualify either but we prefer our soccer on skates with a much smaller pitch and added violence. Even so there may have been the odd craft brew downed in Tronna after the final day of CONCACAF qualifying. The USA just needed a draw. Even if they didn't get it they only needed one of Panama and Honduras not to win and both were losing at half-time. But the US team did not draw and Honduras came from behind to beat Mexico. Meanwhile in Panama, referee Señor Walter López started hallucinating and awarded a goal – not only was the whole of the ball not over the line, not even a quarter of an inch of it was. I'm not even sure it was in the six-yard box! Referee is 'árbitro' in Spanish and that sounds close to arbitrary. Panama's late winner to follow...well, we Canadians are rather polite but let's just say it made me smile.

Soccer isn't a priority to Canada but we do have the best team in North America. This is in terms of standard, in terms of support at the stadium and also in terms of the ability to have a proper name. So the football team from Toronto is called Toronto FC. Not 'Revolution', 'Union', 'Galaxy', 'Earthquakes', 'Wednesday' or any other silly name. Sooner or later our seriousness will feed through into international football and we will qualify ahead of the USA. And when it does we will tip our Panama hats to our southerly neighbours and say, 'that'll teach you to keep winning the Stanley Cup, eh, buddy?!'

A View from North America 3: The USA, but (Actually) Seriously This Time

Patrick Devitt supports Bournemouth and Hereford, and despite his US allegiance that was enough for us to take him seriously. This is what he had to say:

> Am I absolutely shocked that the USA didn't qualify for the World Cup? No. Am I devastated that the US failed to make the World Cup? No. Will this be the death of soccer in the US like some have predicted due to non-qualification? No. Does the USSF need an overhaul? Yes. Can the US become a player on the global scale in football? Yes. I think for this to happen we need our best youth to go abroad and get the best coaching and training that Europe has to offer. The MLS, NASL, or USL don't have the finances or the infrastructure to have quality or sustainable academies to produce elite talented youth players.

Neat summary. So what went wrong this time, then?

> First the results, obviously. There was a poor start to the final qualification round. Under Jürgen Klinsmann they lost their opener at home to Mexico (1-2) and were hammered by Costa Rica (4-0) away. Those were the final nails in Klinsmann's coffin as the USSF brought back Bruce Arena to help right the ship. Sure enough a 6-0 thrashing of Honduras and a 1-1 draw away to Panama eased worries. Further optimism followed with Trinidad and Tobago dispatched 2-0 and a point gained at the Estadio Azteca after a 1-1 draw with Mexico. The next game was a disappointing home loss to Costa Rica, but thereafter a late equalizer in Honduras and 4-0 home trouncing of the hopeful Panamanians put Team USA in the driving seat vis-à-vis its closest rivals for the third qualifying spot. After that, though, the US team simply took its eye off the ball – literally. OK, so in the final games no one

expected Honduras to come from behind to beat Mexico or for the referee to hallucinate in Panama City, but the States just needed a point against Trinidad and Tobago and none of that would have mattered. T&T not TNT! Ranked 80th in the world, with a population of around 1.3 million and a GDP around 1/1000th of that of the United States of America. Eight losses in nine previous qualifying games. Let that all sink in. Final Score: Trinidad and Tobago 2-1 USA.

But soccer, err football, can be like that. Sounds like the USA were unlucky?

Maybe, but I think US Soccer needs a home. England played all of their home qualification matches at Wembley. In contrast, the United States played their five home matches in the final round of qualification in five different cities (Columbus OH, San José CA, Harrison NJ, Commerce City CO, and Orlando FL). What kind of advantage do you have when you play your home matches wherever the USSF decides to have them? This is a massive disadvantage even if it's not obviously seen. Cross-country travel by airplane does take a toll on the body.

You may be right, Pat, and England doesn't have such lengthy travel issues, but since Wembley was rebuilt this century, England has played many games outside London. So just for you, I calculated their fixed home record (matches in London) versus their non-London record with matches in the North East (Newcastle, Sunderland and Middlesbrough), North (Leeds), North West (Liverpool and Manchester), Midlands (Derby and Birmingham), East (Ipswich) and South (Southampton). None yet at the Vitality Stadium or Edgar Street. And so the results for England home matches 2000 to February 2018:

Venue	Played	Won	Drawn	Lost	Points per game*
London	64	42	12	10	2.15
Not London	33	24	6	3	2.36

* Based on 3 for a win, 1 for a draw, regardless of whether friendly or competitive

Two of England's away defeats came at its next most used/large venue of Old Trafford. Not sure this proves very much, and granted, it is a massive tangent from World Cup qualification, but is there anything else to say?

The final point is to say there is light at the end of the tunnel: Christian Pulisic. The "golden boy of US soccer" was the team's lone hope towards the end of qualification. However, that in itself is a problem; our best player was just a kid. Don't get me wrong, Pulisic is a supremely talented player, and I will add that he made the best decision he could have by going overseas to play in Germany for Dortmund, but he is still a kid. He led scoring (five goals) but also struggled with the physicality of the games; even so, no one else for the US really took their game to another level. More or less the plan was for Pulisic to create chances for Pulisic to score. There was no plan B.

Ah, 'Plan Le Tissier', as it is known, after he kept Southampton in the English top division for nigh on a decade in the 1990s.

Yes, well, like that Saints team, the players we have now for the most part aren't good enough or their best days are behind them. We have some good players in the youth ranks, but the best athletes in the US aren't playing soccer; they're playing American football or basketball. I think it will be extremely hard to compete on a global level when the best of the best athletes that we produce have no interest in 'soccer'. This is a much deeper issue that we don't have time for so I will wrap this up.

OK, many thanks, Patrick, but money, size of population and the fact that 'soccer' is a much better game than baseball and 'gridiron' should mean that Team USA is back for Qatar.

A View From The Netherlands: Pass the Dutchie

So is it Holland or Nederlands? One thing's for sure, if a nation was going to find something to disagree about in footballing terms it is the Dutch, so having different names is not a surprise. You might have expected to see them in Russia. Having narrowly lost a World Cup final for the third time in 2010, they started the 2014 tournament by thrashing champions Spain 5-1, including a Van Persie wonder goal and despite being 1-0 down. They were one of four teams with a 100% record, and the only team to get into double figures for goals, in the group stages. They started the knockout stages, however, in less than inspiring form, needing two late goals. The second was a penalty deep into injury time, converted by Huntelaar, won by Tom Daley.[2] After that they needed a penalty win after drawing 0-0 with Costa Rica (see, anyone can do it) to reach the semi-finals, where they also drew 0-0, this time losing the shoot-out to Argentina. The campaign and perhaps the 'end of era' squad had run out of steam, even if they did beat Brazil 3-0 to finish third. Even so, they did not make it to Russia, finding themselves in a qualifying group with Sweden and France. So what are we to make of Dutch football? I asked Rod

---

[2] Obviously Arjen Robben, but the dive was that good.

Besseling (aka Goldmember) who agreed to talk to me for the sum of one *million dollars*. Here are his rather downbeat[3] thoughts on the orange machine.

It didn't really come as a surprise, but still, it's a shame that the orange fans won't be in Russia; it could do with a colour that isn't grey. We have to acknowledge, however, that the Dutch national team has recently played some of the dullest, low intensity football the world has ever seen. Untotal Football in Orwellian Newspeak. It felt like a health and safety expert had taken over as manager. It was sort of football, but with the stabilizers still on. So how did we finish third at the last one only to fail to make it to Moscow?

Frankly, the warning signs were already there and the Iron Tulip (van Gaal) performed some kind of miracle in Brazil given the very un-Dutch style of football based on opportunistic counter-attacking. Supporters and commentators didn't seem to question the tactics (so long as we won!) and no one seemed to notice the 'second death' of Cruyff. After the tournament, players were purchased by top clubs around Europe but almost all failed to live up to expectation. Many came to the Premier League and even where they didn't fail, failed to set the league alight: Jordy Classie, Memphis Depay, Eljero Elia, Vincent Jansen, Luuk de Jong, Jermaine Lens and Ricky van Wolfswinkel (great name, mind you). Others have done better but have hardly been spectacular: Ibrahim Afellay, Daley Blind, Leroy Fer, Daryl Janmaat, Davy Klaassen and Georgie Wijnadum. Where a Dutch player was once seen as a sound investment, who would deliver at the highest level, the current crop of players seem to have tricked the world into thinking they were good. And to be fair, they were good (in the Dutch league). Most

---

[3] He doesn't use the word 'hup' even once.

worryingly, it's not only the players; managers are losing the plot too. Louis van Gaal (Manchester United), Dick Advocaat (Sunderland), Ronald Koeman (Everton) and Ronald de Boer (Crystal Palace).

A lot of this concerns the playing style that is being promoted and played in the Netherlands. We are world champions of passive possession. As Michiel de Hoog stated, 'we are the panda of European Football: apathetic, unexciting and you just can't get any drive in the team'. For the Dutch, it's all about ball control and passing and being safe; completely risk adverse. No turns. No trick penalties. The Dutch football can be seen as a form of continuous foreplay. No Ruud Krol thunderbolts. No Ruudness or Gullitness at all. No orgasmic Van Basten volleys.

The solution should be easy! More direct passes and pass the ball forward. Problem is, possession football is very deep in Dutch footballing culture. We have a pathological love for possession. The Dutch top flight, the Eredivisie, is the most sterile competition in Europe. We should be calling it Das Eredivisie, champions of possession for the sake of having possession, not because we are planning on doing anything with it.

But there is hope. All is not lost. We have the Dutch women's team. In 2017, our proud lionesses ended the German reign in the UEFA Women's championship and became European Champions. They played with passion, pride and drive, everything the men's team is missing. The games were exciting, emotional and real. These professional athletes had the passion to win for their nation and they made all of us proud. The men's team can learn a thing or two from them.

So where does this leave us for the men's team? Well, this is going to take at least a generation to fix.[4] We need to address the structural problems and re-boot from the grassroots level up. Over the past decade, Spain, France and even our southern neighbours, Belgium, structurally and culturally altered their playing styles and adopted a high-tempo, pressure and forward-looking game. We have the talent in the Netherlands...I mean, if Belgium does,[5] surely we do as well...we just lack the adequate coaching talent, leadership and direction to foster these young players with a winning mentality.

For the sake of making ourselves feel better, having not qualified for Russia 2018 let's preempt our future failure by saying we will boycott Qatar 2022 due to mistreatment of mainly migrant workers building the infrastructure, and that we will focus all our attention and energy on the 2026 World Cup. Surely our impotent team and managers will have rediscovered their drive at this point, if only by following the lead of our women.

A View from Italy: No Comment

Of course no one from Italy was available for comment and I wouldn't intrude on their enormous collective grief to ask for one. I noticed over the years, though, that Italy often trod the line very precisely. They would get through finals groups on goals scored (or sometimes miss out), they would settle for penalties (and sometimes lose) and they would beat Malta 1-0 in qualifying, home and away. And yet they have managed to win the World Cup four times, making them by far the most successful team in Europe,

---

[4] This is generally the case with Dutch football.

[5] It's a bit like if you added to England doing badly in Russia (as we surely will) Scotland suddenly reaching the semis. Thankfully not a problem we have.

since Westgermany (three wins) will presumably not win it again. And though I am not angry at Italy, I do think that 'the beautiful game' ceased to be so when someone Italian noticed that it is not the team that scores the most goals which wins football matches, but the team which concedes the fewest; not the prettiest, but the dirtiest. So, if this non-qualification causes at least a partial re-evaluation of how the game should be played, in Italy as well as Holland, this may be a blessing in disguise, eh, *ragazzi*?

Conclusions: The Future

So, there is very little to do now but wait and fill in the results in the fixture pages that follow. We hope you enjoy. If this book hasn't gone overboard about Russia as a World Cup location, that has been nothing compared to the general downer on the award to Qatar for 2022. I mean, surely Australia would have been better, for football, for supporters, for FIFA? But looking forward – as we must after England disappoints again – David Harding, who lives and works in Doha, offered to tell us why it might not be as bad as we think.

It's not impossible to imagine this as a football supporter: you are going to love the Qatar World Cup. The group stage will see four games a day, which means you can spend the whole day watching the best players in the world play. Furthermore, the tournament will be shorter than normal – spread out over just 28 days compared to 32 in Russia – which means there shouldn't be any of those awful moments when play stops for a whole 24 hours. And Qatar is just three hours ahead of Greenwich Mean Time, which means that for many places all the games will be played at amenable hours.

By switching the tournament to Northern Hemisphere winter time, the 2022 World Cup will also finish on December 18. So, instead of that usual empty feeling straight after the end of a World Cup, you can slide straight into Christmas. Turkey for your cold turkey. If you are an old-school fan who actually goes to matches, flight times to Doha are between six and seven hours long from London, Paris or Berlin, the same as getting to Ekaterinburg, one of the Russia 2018 venues. Once you get there, the longest distance to travel between grounds is about an hour's drive. It all means that from November 21, 2022, when the event kicks off in the 80,000-seat Lusail Stadium, through to January 1, you have to think of little other than football and the Holidays. Wonderful.

Of course, this all goes against the narrative of the Qatar World Cup, largely touted as a moral disgrace and an indelible stain on the competition. Since – incomprehensibly – FIFA chose/was paid (delete according to viewpoint) to select desert country Qatar as host, initially in the summer, no event in sporting history has become so controversial. And certainly no event has been so criticised. Qatar has faced widespread allegations of corruption, human rights abuse, and even supporting terrorism as part of the constant crisis surrounding 2022. Critics suggest some 1,200 World Cup workers have been killed preparing the country for the tournament – and many more will follow.

Qatar has been dismissed as a country with no football tradition, which has just used its oil money (most of its incredible wealth is actually down to gas) to pay its way to sit at football's top table. You can add that to the claims that alcohol and gay fans will be banned during the competition. In just a few years since winning the right to host and proving itself to be one of the most ambitious countries on the planet, Qatar's name has been continually dragged through the mud. It has gone from being a country who many had not even heard of, or thought was part of the UAE, to one that is now a byword for modern-day slavery. Can anywhere really be that bad?

One thing that won't be a factor is the weather. Temperatures in Qatar's summer can reach more than 120 degrees Fahrenheit, 50 degrees Celsius. When the sun goes down the humidity goes up. It is a sweaty, stifling, horrible heat. November and December, meanwhile, are more likely to be around 80F degrees/ 28C, cloudy, windy; it will probably even rain. When the Qataris use their famous air-conditioning technology in the stadiums, you might have to take a coat to keep warm.

Corruption charges are a far less easy to shake off. Qatar is under investigation in Switzerland for how it won the 2022 bid, a process which could theoretically see Doha lose the World Cup, though this is unlikely. Its name is to the fore again in a trial of former FIFA executives/gangsters in New York. It's hard to imagine how anyone would agree to staging a World Cup in a desert in the summer – which was the case originally – without stuffed envelopes playing a part. But if Qatar is somewhere found guilty of corruption, it will not be so in isolation. What such a verdict would prove is football's fetid core, not one country acting alone.

On workers' rights, Qatar has made its first move to improve. It has agreed to a whole package of reforms, notably a minimum wage and allowing workers to leave their contracts and the country if they choose to. These are only promises at the moment, but they have definitely given critics some hope. The safety record, though, remains sketchy. On World Cup projects there have so far, officially, been three deaths attributed to accidents. The number of workers killed across all infrastructure projects – and it is easy to make the case that the whole of Qatar, which is spending $500m a week on the World Cup, is being built or rebuilt for 2022 – is unknown. Qatar doesn't help itself with a lack of transparency over figures and public announcements on causes of death. There may not have been 1,200 people killed but the truth is no one knows what the true figure is.

Maybe the biggest threat to the competition is the current Gulf Crisis, a political stand-off between countries in the region which has seen Qatar isolated by its neighbours and may even see the competition boycotted if the dispute drags on long enough. That would be a big hit for Qatar – the majority of the 1.5m fans expected to attend in 2022 will come from the region, many from Saudi Arabia, giving the World Cup a totally different flavour to previous events. It would also fatally undermine Qatar's often-stated aim to unite the region through football. There is tremendous pride that 2022 will be the first Middle East World Cup, but that would be scuppered by a regional boycott. There has been a lot of anger at the Western narrative – dismissed as racism by some – concentrating on Qatar's labour rights record, but local shunning would be worse for the tournament.

As for alcohol – it will be available during the World Cup. Qatar is a conservative, Muslim country, but not one with a booze-ban. The sale of drink is strictly limited, sold in hotels and to ex-pats with an alcohol licence. During the World Cup it will be available but strictly regulated. How Qatar deals with a load of fans in what is essentially a one-city country is a great unknown. It is a safe, clean, modern country but it is not exactly a party place. It has never dealt with the sheer volume of fans it will receive in 2022. Homosexuality is banned in Qatar but organisers have said that for the World Cup, everyone will be welcome to attend, regardless. That may not sound like the friendliest or most inclusive, liberal statement.

And after all that, what about its football team? Qatar has spent billions on trying to qualify for a World Cup and develop players. So far, it has managed very little and is ranked 102nd in the world. But there are signs of life, the dead wood is being cut from the side, the young players are being pushed through and by 2022 if Qatar is not managed by Xavi Hernández, it will be managed by Pep Guardiola. The national side – the al-Annabi (the maroons) – will probably surprise everyone and qualify for the second round, which might be further than England gets.

So not exactly unequivocal support, but at least there is some positive analysis there, even if, when push comes to shove, I cannot imagine that we will bother with a guide-book for Qatar at all. Although since you'll all be busy doing your Christmas shopping...

Appendix:

Groups, Fixtures and Results

You'll have to do the results yourselves, obviously.

GROUPS

Group A

Despite being hosts, Russia still got a draw in which all the teams were above them in the FIFA world rankings. Oh yes, that's because all the other 31 teams *are* above them, including Saudi Arabia, whom they play first. The group is made up of Egypt and Uruguay. Uruguay ought to be favourites, but all the teams will feel they have a chance.

Group B

A tightly-clustered group geographically, with Portugal and Spain being drawn with their southern neighbour Morocco. Iran make up the quartet and will be tough to break down, as they proved in qualifying. Although Spain and Portugal ought to cruise through, if either of them wins the first game between them the other will be under a lot of pressure. Although this is a golden generation of Moroccan football, they are likely to struggle.

Group C

France are clear favourites, but expect the team spirit of the other teams to be decisive. Australia are playing in their fourth successive finals; having struggled to get there, they will want more from the finals. Peru are looking to put 36 years of hurt behind them and ranked in FIFA's top ten; and Denmark have Erikssen. All the non-French teams qualified through play-offs and will be determined and battle-hardened by the process.

Group D

Argentina 0 Iceland 1. It's not a prediction, but I hope to be able to type it again someday for real. Croatia and Nigeria both have their good days, but probably not enough of them. The crazy ice warriors might just do it again, you know.

Group E

Brazil will struggle...to make this look like hard work. More flamboyant than the Swiss, bigger than the Ticos and less Tadicey than the Serbs, this group looks like a battle for second place which will probably be won by Switzerland.

Group F

Germany, Mexico, Sweden and South Korea. Of course, the Germans have struggled in Russia before, but not at football. The game between Mexico and Sweden will probably be the decisive one with two entirely contrasting teams; physique, technique, psychologique. Ibrahimović to be tripped up by his own ego at the decisive moment?

Group G

Belgium, Panama, Tunisia and England. Sky's computer predicted England had only just got a better than half chance of getting out of the group (53%), and only just better than a quarter chance of reaching the last eight. Fewer than two-thirds of even England fans thought they would get out of the group. This sense of realism could help take pressure off the team. Playing Belgium last could be crucial as even a draw or two in the opening games might be enough if they can win that one. And as we know, England are capable of losing to, or beating, anyone on their day. The draw looks to have been kind to the economy, by scheduling matches when fewest people will have to throw a sicky.

Group H

Poland cannot believe their luck, having been drawn against Senegal, Colombia and Japan. Senegal cannot believe their luck, having been drawn against Poland, Colombia and Japan. Colombia cannot believe their luck, having been drawn against Poland, Senegal and Japan. Japan cannot believe their luck, having been drawn against Poland, Senegal and Colombia. All of them cannot believe their luck that one of them may be just a game against England away from a quarter-final.

FIXTURES

(and scribble in your own results)

GROUP STAGE

Thursday 14 June

Group A

Russia	v	Saudi Arabia
	Luzhniki Stadium	
	Moscow	
	Kick-off: 16.00	

Scorers:

Friday 15 June

Group A

Egypt	v	Uruguay

Ekaterinburg
Stadium

Ekaterinburg

Kick-off:
13.00

Scorers:

Group B

Morocco	v	Iran

Saint Petersburg
Stadium

St. Petersburg

Kick-off:
16.00

Scorers:

Group B

Portugal   v   Spain

Fisht Stadium

Sochi

Kick-off:
19.00

Scorers:

Saturday 16 June

Group C

France   v   Australia

Kazan Arena

Kazan

Kick-off:
11.00

Scorers:

Group D

Argentina   v   Iceland

Otkrytiye Arena

Moscow

Kick-off:
14.00

Scorers:

Group C

Peru   v   Denmark

Saransk Stadium

Saransk

Kick-off:
17.00

Scorers:

Group D

Croatia
v
Nigeria

Kaliningrad
Stadium

Kaliningrad

Kick-off:
20.00

Scorers:

Sunday 17 June

Group E

Costa Rica
v
Serbia

Samara Stadium

Samara

Kick-off:
13.00

Scorers:

Group F

Germany   v   Mexico

Luzhniki Stadium

Moscow

Kick-off:
16.00

Scorers:

Group E

Brazil   v   Switzerland

Rostov-on-Don Stadium

Rostov-on-Don

Kick-off:
19.00

Scorers:

Monday 18 June

Group P

Sweden	v	Korea Republic

Nizhny Novgorod Stadium

Nizhny Novgorod

Kick-off:
13.00

Scorers:

Group G

Belgium	v	Panama

Fisht Stadium

Sochi

Kick-off:
16.00

Scorers:

Group G

Tunisia	v	England

Volgograd
Stadium

Volgograd

Kick-off:
19.00

Scorers:

Tuesday 19 June

Group H

Poland	v	Senegal

Otkrytiye Arena

Moscow

Kick-off:
13.00

Scorers:

Group H

Colombia   v   Japan

Saransk
Stadium

Saransk

Kick-off:
16.00

Scorers:

Group A

Russia   v   Egypt

Saint Petersburg
Stadium

St. Petersburg

Kick-off:
19.00

Scorers:

Wednesday 20 June

Group B

Portugal   v   **Morocco**

Luzhniki Stadium

Moscow

Kick-off:
13.00

Scorers:

Group A

Uruguay   v   **Saudi Arabia**

Rostov-on-Don
Stadium

Rostov-on-Don

Kick-off:
16.00

Scorers:

Group B

Iran   v   ## Spain

Kazan Arena

Kazan

Kick-off:
19.00

Scorers:

Thursday 21 June

Group C

France   v   ## Peru

Ekaterinburg
Stadium

Ekaterinburg

Kick-off:
13.00

Scorers:

Group C

Denmark	v	**Australia**
	Samara Stadium	
	Samara	
	Kick-off: 16.00	

Scorers:

Group D

Argentina	v	**Croatia**
	Nizhny Novgorod Stadium	
	Nizhny Novgorod	
	Kick-off: 19.00	

Scorers:

Friday 22 June

Group E

Brazil	v	Costa Rica

Saint Petersburg Stadium

Saint Petersburg

Kick-off:
13.00

Scorers:

Group D

Nigeria	v	Iceland

Volgograd Stadium

Volgograd

Kick-off:
16.00

Scorers:

Group E

Serbia   v   Switzerland

Kaliningrad Stadium

Kaliningrad

Kick-off:
19.00

Scorers:

Saturday 23 June

Group G

Belgium   v   Tunisia

Otkrytiye Arena

Moscow

Kick-off:
13.00

Scorers:

Group F

Germany   v   Sweden

Fisht Stadium

Sochi

Kick-off:
16.00

Scorers:

Group F

Korea Republic   v   Mexico

Rostov-on-Don
Stadium

Rostov-on-Don

Kick-off:
19.00

Scorers:

Sunday 24 June

Group G

England   v   **Panama**

Nizhny Novgorod
Stadium

Nizhny Novgorod

Kick-off:
13.00

Scorers:

Group F

Japan   v   **Senegal**

Ekaterinburg
Stadium

Ekaterinburg

Kick-off:
16.00

Scorers:

Group H

Poland v Colombia

Kazan Arena

Kazan

Kick-off:
19.00

Scorers:

Monday 25 June

Group A

Uruguay v Russia

Samara Stadium

Samara

Kick-off:
15.00

Scorers:

Group A

Saudi Arabia　　　v　　　Egypt

Volgograd Stadium

Volgograd

Kick-off:
15.00

Scorers:

Group B

Iran　　　v　　　Portugal

Saransk Stadium

Saransk

Kick-off:
19.00

Scorers:

Group B

Spain	v	Morocco

Kaliningrad Stadium

Kaliningrad

Kick-off:
19.00

Scorers:

Tuesday 26 June

Group C

Denmark	v	France

Luzhniki Stadium

Moscow

Kick-off:
15.00

Scorers:

Group C

Australia	v	Peru
	Fisht Stadium	
	Sochi	
	Kick-off:	
	15.00	

Scorers:

Group D

Nigeria	v	Argentina
	Saint Petersburg Stadium	
	Saint Petersburg	
	Kick-off:	
	19.00	

Scorers:

Group D

Iceland	v	Croatia

Rostov-on-Don
Stadium

Rostov-on-Don

Kick-off:
19.00

Scorers:

Wednesday 27 June

Group F

Mexico	v	Sweden

Ekaterinburg
Stadium

Ekaterinburg

Kick-off:
15.00

Scorers:

Group F

Korea Republic   v   **Germany**

Kazan Arena

Kazan

Kick-off:
15.00

Scorers:

Group E

Serbia   v   **Brazil**

Otkrytiye Arena

Moscow

Kick-off:

19.00

Scorers:

Group E

Switzerland	v	Costa Rica

Nizhny Novgorod
Stadium

Nizhny Novgorod

Kick-off:
19.00

Scorers:

Thursday 28 June

Group H

Japan	v	Poland

Volgograd Stadium

Volgograd

Kick-off:
15.00

Scorers:

Group H

Senegal　　　　v　　　　**Colombia**

Samara Stadium

Samara

Kick-off:
15.00

Scorers:

Group G

Panama　　　　v　　　　**Tunisia**

Saransk Stadium

Saransk

Kick-off:
19.00

Scorers:

Group G

England   v   Belgium

Kaliningrad Stadium

Kaliningrad

Kick-off:
19.00

Scorers:

ROUND OF 16

Saturday 30 June

Match 1

[1C]   v   [2D]

Kazan Arena

Kazan

Kick-off:
15.00

Winner QF1:

Scorers:

Match 2

[1A]   v   [2B]

Fisht Stadium

Sochi

Kick-off:
19.00

Winner QF2:

Scorers:

Match 3

[1B]   v   [2A]

Luzhniki Stadium

Moscow

Kick-off:
15.00

Winner QF3:

Scorers:

Match 4

[1D]　　　　　　　v　　　　　　　[2C]

Nizhny Novgorod
Stadium

Nizhny Novgorodi

Kick-off:
19.00

Winner QF4:

Scorers:

Match 5

[1E]　　　　　　　v　　　　　　　[2F]

Samara Stadium

Samara

Kick-off:
15.00

Winner QF5:

Scorers:

Match 6

[1G]   v   [2H]

**Rostov-on-Don
Stadium**

Rostov-on-Don

**Kick-off:
19.00**

Winner QF6:

Scorers:

Match 7

[1F]   v   [2E]

**Saint Petersburg
Stadium**

Saint Petersburg

**Kick-off:
15.00**

Winner QF7:

Scorers:

Match 8

[1H]   **v**   [2G]

Otkrytiye Arena

Moscow

Kick-off:
19.00

Winner QF8:

Scorers:

QUARTER-FINALS

Match 1

[QF1]   v   [QF2]

Nizhny Novgorod
Stadium

Nizhny Novgorod

Kick-off:
15.00

Winner QF1:

Scorers:

Match 2

[QF5]   v   [QF6]

Kazan Arena

Kazan

Kick-off:
19.00

Winner QF2:

Scorers:

Saturday 07 July

Match 3

[QF7]   v   [QF8]

Samara Stadium

Samara

Kick-off:
13.00

Winner QF3:

Scorers:

Match 4

[QF3]   v   [QF4]

Fisht Stadium

Sochi

Kick-off:
19.00

Winner QF4:

Scorers:

SEMI-FINALS

Semi-final 1

[QF1] v [QF2]

Saint Petersburg
Stadium

Saint Petersburg

Kick-off:
19.00

Winner SF1:

Scorers:

Wednesday 11 July

Semi-final 2

[QF3] v [QF4]

Luzhniki Stadium

Moscow

Kick-off:
19.00

Winner SF2:

Scorers:

Round for irrelevant losers which no-one wants to play in except perhaps the young lad that was brought along for the experience and the reserve goal-keeper who otherwise wouldn't have got a look in.

THIRD-PLACE PLAY OFF

Saturday 14 July

[SF1]   v   [SF2]

Saint Petersburg
Stadium

Saint Petersburg

Kick-off:
15.00

Winner Third Place:

Scorers:

FINAL

[England[1]]   **v**   [SF2]

Luzhniki Stadium

Moscow

Kick-off:
16.00

Winner:

Scorers:

---

[1] There is, apparently a 4.7% chance of this happening, so we may as well pop it in, eh?

About the Authors

Lloyd Pettiford

Born in Manchester in the year England last won the World Cup. This is the 26th book Lloyd has written and the 7th on football. In previous blurbs he has gone with different motifs: sentimental, accurate, surreal and plain waffly. For this one – which the publisher asked for at a time of great hangover - he simply wishes to scotch the rumour (which he admittedly started) that he once took penalties for Dulwich Hamlet (Reserves). Oh and to ask very nicely if you wouldn't mind buying the book? Please.

Ronan Fitzsimons

Originally from the North East of England, Ronan leads a double life: by day, he is a respectable university lecturer who talks codswallop to his bewildered but touchingly loyal students; in his spare time he writes balderdash on a range of topics for the benefit of his baffled but touchingly loyal readership. He enjoys co-authoring books with Lloyd Pettiford as the process allows him to come up with third-rate puns, anagrams and celebrity double-lookalikes with robust justification.

World Cup 2018

HAVE YOU ENJOYED WORLD CUP 2018?

Why not try *The Premier League: 25 Years....*

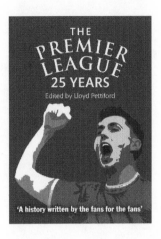

The 2016/17 season marked the 25th of the Premier League. This book recognises that fact in a way which is factually accurate yet dismissive of reputations and hype. It recognises the achievements of Swindon and Barnsley as much as Manchester United and Chelsea, and sneaks in references to Borg drones from Star Trek, Oscar Wilde, Nirvana and Red Dwarf alongside analysis of the songs and seasons. Notts County fan Billy Ivory's foreword sets a tone of bitter irony as the story (shocked back to life by Leicester City) is told in unconventional fashion. Fans of all 49 teams who've been involved in Premier League have their say, except for Huddersfield (due to publishing deadlines), although we feel sure Patrick Stewart will want this one for Christmas...The Premier League charts each of the 25 seasons with the story of how the titles were won and the players who starred. From 2011/12's incredible finale, to Arsenal's "Invincibles", as well as each of Manchester United's record 13 triumphs, find out more about the rich history of the Premier League.

URBANE

Urbane Publications is dedicated to
developing new author voices, and publishing
fiction and non-fiction that challenges, thrills and
fascinates. From page-turning novels to innovative
reference books, our goal is to publish what
YOU want to read.

Find out more at

urbanepublications.com